WHAT THE **BIBLE** TEACHES ABOUT

A N G E L S

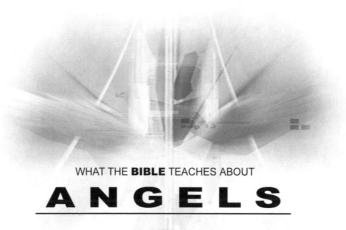

WHAT THE **BIBLE** TEACHES ABOUT

A N G E L S

ROGER ELLSWORTH

EVANGELICAL PRESS

EVANGELICAL PRESS
Faverdale North, Darlington, DL3 0PH, England

e-mail: sales@evangelicalpress.org

Evangelical Press USA
P. O. Box 825, Webster, New York 14580, USA

e-mail: usa.sales@evangelicalpress.org

web: http://www.evangelicalpress.org

Second Impression 2007

British Library Cataloguing in Publication Data available

ISBN-13   978-0-85234-617-4   ISBN 0-85234-617-4

Printed and bound in the United States of America.

*The following pages are dedicated
to my dear friends and fellow servants,
Lanny Faulkner and Don Whitney*

Acknowledgements

My sincere thanks go to David Clark and Bob Dickie for inviting me to participate in the *What the Bible teaches about...* series. It is, I judge, much needed, and I trust that under the good hand of our God will accomplish much good.

I also appreciate the congregation of Immanuel Baptist Church eagerly listening to the series of sermons from which this book came. These dear saints are a constant blessing to their pastor!

As always, I am deeply indebted to my wife Sylvia for her steady encouragement and simply for sharing the journey. Thanks, dear heart!

Contents

Introduction

People are interested in angels. If asked, they could give several reasons for that interest. But often those same people are not quite so clear on why they should be interested in the Bible.

The Bible itself answers the question. We should be interested in it because it is no ordinary book. Its own testimony is that it is God's book. Its teachings are true and timeless because its author is the eternal God. Yes, men wrote the Bible, but they were not left to themselves. They were rather men whom the Spirit of the Lord caught up and carried along to the point that the words they wrote were the words of God (2 Timothy 3:16-17; 2 Peter 1:19-21).

The Lord Jesus Christ himself bore witness to the truth of Scripture on more than one occasion (Matthew 4:4; 5:17-18; John 5:39; 10:34-36). He told the Sadducees that they were 'greatly mistaken' in their denial of the resurrection because they did not know the Scriptures (Mark 12:24, 27).

And the Lord Jesus proved for ever his authority to speak about the authority of Scripture by his own resurrection. This astounding event showed him to be 'the Son of God with power' (Romans 1:4).

The subject of angels gives us plenty of room to be as 'greatly mistaken' as the Sadducees. But if we will pay careful heed to Scripture, we can avoid the mistakes and come to the truth.

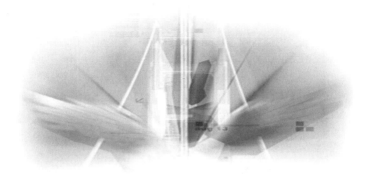

1. The God of the angels

Please read: Psalm 103:20-22; 148:1-6

Movies, television shows, figurines, books, magazine articles and seminars — angels are everywhere!

This would seem to be very good news. After all, the Bible does have a lot to say about angels, mentioning them 273 times. Should we not welcome such widespread interest in a biblical topic?

Yet interest in a biblical topic is of no value if we are not biblical about the topic. All too often, the only connection between the current angel-mania and the Bible is the teaching that angels exist. In other words, the Bible takes us in an entirely different direction on the matter of angels than the current obsession with them. The latter is often nothing more than an attempt to get around God. An article in *Time* magazine put it like this: 'For those who choke too easily on God and his rules … angels are the handy compromise, all fluff and meringue, kind, nonjudgemental. They are available to everyone, like aspirin.'[1]

But the Bible takes us in exactly the opposite direction. It teaches us about the angels so that we will adore the God of the angels. The angels ought to drive us to him.

What do the angels teach us about God? Wonderful things indeed! We will now mention four such things.

The strength of God

Consider the strength of the angels. David says they 'excel in strength' (Psalm 103:20). What does this say about God? Psalm 148:5 declares that he is their Creator. Is not the Creator greater than the creature? If then the angels excel in strength, how much more does God excel in strength.

Consider the number of angels. How many angels are there? Hebrews 12:22 says they are 'innumerable'. Revelation 5:11 says there are 'ten thousand times ten thousand, and thousands of thousands'. David Jeremiah offers this explanation: 'To give you a perspective on how many angels this is, the average football stadium in America holds about 50,000 people. It would take some 2,000 stadiums of that size to hold 100,000,000 people. The total number of angels John saw may have far exceeded 100,000,000.'[2]

We must remember that God created all these angels. How great is he that he could create such a multitude of these beings! We are face to face again with the strength of almighty God who does his creating by merely speaking (Psalm 148:5)!

How much strength does God have? There is no way to calculate it. This much is sure — he has enough strength to save, to keep and to bless his people. He is strong enough to deal with their problems and strong enough to finally bring them home to heaven!

The wisdom of God

Let us think for a moment about the various types of angels. In addition to an archangel, the Bible identifies cherubim and seraphim.

◇◇◇◇◇◇◇◇◇◇◇◇◇◇◇◇◇◇◇◇◇◇◇◇

The Bible

teaches us

about the angels

so that

we will adore

the God

of the angels.

◇◇◇◇◇◇◇◇◇◇◇◇◇◇◇◇◇◇◇◇◇◇◇◇

So far as we can tell there is only one archangel. His name is Michael, which is revealed in Jude 9.

The *cherubim*, described in Ezekiel 1:4-14, 22-26, are closely associated with the holy presence of God.

Seraphim are described in the opening verses of Isaiah 6.

In addition to these, the Bible mentions thrones, dominions, principalities and powers (Ephesians 6:12; Colossians 1:16).

My purpose at this point is not to go into detail about the various types of angels but rather to draw attention again to the God who made them. Yes, the different kinds of angels underscore again the strength of God. But they also take us to his wisdom. How very wise he must be to be able to make such a variety of beings!

How wise is God? He is certainly wise enough to plan and to secure the salvation of his people. And he is wise enough to guide his people through all their trials and afflictions.

The lovingkindness of God

Some would have us believe that God made the world only to leave it to itself. According to them, he made it and walked away! But Psalm 103:21 says the angels are 'ministers' of God 'who do his pleasure'. Hebrews 1:14 says they are 'ministering spirits' who 'minister for those who will inherit eternal salvation'.

The Bible abounds with instances such as these. An angel encouraged Gideon (Judges 6:12). An angel gave guidance to Joseph (Matthew 2:19-20). An angel gave directions to Philip (Acts 8:26). An angel boarded a ship to encourage Paul (Acts 27:23-24). An angel even strengthened the Lord Jesus in his humanity (Luke 22:43).

An angel hastened a saint out of a doomed city. Another wrestled with a saint. Another appeared to a donkey and caused a prophet to act like a donkey. Another baked a cake for another prophet. Another protected a man of God from becoming lunch for lions. Another engineered a jailbreak for an apostle.

On the basis of these and other events, one commentator concluded that angels protect, guide, encourage, deliver, enlighten and empower us.[3]

But that runs the risk of giving the angels too much credit. It is God who used the angels to do these things. The angels are his agents to accomplish his will. He is ever and always the source of our every blessing — not the angels themselves!

The worthiness of God to receive our obedience and praise

The angels obey God. They 'do his word, heeding the voice of his word' (Psalm 103:20). They also 'do his pleasure' (Psalm 103:21).

We know that the angels are capable of disobedience. As we shall have occasion to note, Lucifer led one third of the original number in an ill-fated rebellion against God. But the angels who did not join in that rebellion evidently learned lessons from it and now serve God faithfully.

Like the angels, we are called to heed God's word. We are to be 'doers of the word' (James 1:22). And like the good angels, we can certainly see that rebellion against God only brings ruin and heartache.

With such knowledge, we also should obey God. The angels obey him promptly, gladly and faithfully. Let us aspire to do the same.

The angels also praise God. They are praising beings (Psalm 103:20-22; 148:2, 5; Revelation 5:11-12; 7:11-12). Yet the truth of the matter is that the angels praise God because they enjoy God. They enjoy the glory of his person and the glory of his works (Job 38:7).

This has immense significance for us. If the angels enjoy God, should we not do the same? If the angels, great as they are, find reason to praise God, should we not be praising him?

15

The author of Hebrews lays the duty of praise before us in these words: '…let us continually offer the sacrifice of praise to God, that is, the fruit of our lips, giving thanks to his name' (Hebrews 13:15).

We certainly have plenty of reasons for praise. God has blessed us in innumerable ways. And he has blessed us with the greatest of all his gifts — eternal life through the redeeming death of his Son (John 3:16).

As we continue this study of the angels, more and more we will find ourselves drawn away from the angels themselves to the God they serve and praise. And as that happens, the angels will be pleased too.

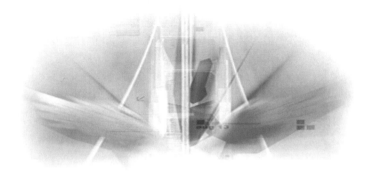

2. The résumé of Lucifer

Please read: Isaiah 14:12-17; Ezekiel 28:11-19

Verses 3-23 of Isaiah 14 constitute a stinging indictment of the king of Babylon, as is clear from verse 4. The king, intoxicated with himself and his glory, would seek to deify himself. And that would bring upon him the crushing judgement of almighty God.

But this Scripture, like so many others, moves on more than one level. While its first application is to the king of Babylon, it quickly becomes apparent that this could not possibly exhaust all that is said here.

We must, therefore, look beyond the king of Babylon to another king. To put it another way, we must look beyond the first level of application to yet another level.

That level takes us to a far greater being than the king of Babylon. It takes us to this beautiful being identified as 'Lucifer' (v. 12), which means 'morning star' or 'day star'.

As we examine this passage, we find that the sin of the king of Babylon — the sin of self-advancement or self-exaltation — was merely the repetition of the sin of Lucifer. He was the first to have committed this sin.

Who was this Lucifer to whom the passage refers? It is none other than the person we now know as Satan ('adversary'). Here we have his résumé. This passage pulls back the curtain and shows us how Satan became Satan.

The original Lucifer

He did not begin in this way. He began as Lucifer. As we have noted, God created all the angels, and he created all kinds of angels. Lucifer was evidently supreme among all of them.

We find in Ezekiel 28:11-15 a passage very similar to the one we have here in Isaiah. That passage also begins with an earthly king, the king of Tyre, but moves to a higher level or to the king behind the king. Just as Satan was the king who stood behind the king of Babylon in Isaiah 14, so he is the king who stood behind the king of Tyre in Ezekiel 28. Here is Ezekiel's description of him:

'You were the seal of perfection,
Full of wisdom and perfect in beauty...
You were the anointed cherub who covers...
You were perfect in your ways from the day you were created...'

(vv. 12, 14, 15).

What a glorious being! Lucifer was filled with wisdom. He was perfect in beauty. He enjoyed a special status: 'the anointed cherub who covers'. Jonathan Edwards says: '...by the covering cherub is meant the cherub next to the throne of God himself, having a place in the very holy of holies'.[1]

Edwards further says: '...before the fall of this cherub he is spoken of as being alone entitled to this great honour and nearness to God's throne in heaven, that he was anointed to be above his fellows'.[2]

The rebellious Lucifer

However, Lucifer did not keep his exalted position. Why was this not possible? Isaiah's prophecy gives the answer in the form of a fivefold 'I'. Lucifer said in his heart:

'I will ascend into heaven,
I will exalt my throne above the stars of God;
I will also sit on the mount of the congregation...
I will ascend above the heights of the clouds,
I will be like the Most High'

(vv. 13-14).

Filled with himself and his own beauty, Lucifer was no longer content to serve the Lord. He would overthrow God and take his place!

Some have offered a more detailed suggestion about the nature of Lucifer's sin. They understand it in terms of God announcing to the angels that he, God, would create mankind, that mankind would fall into sin, and that the second person of the Trinity would take humanity unto himself to redeem mankind. God further announced that all the angels of heaven would be required to worship and serve Christ in his humanity and to serve as ministering spirits to men. And Lucifer could not bear this. He regarded it as being beneath him and rebelled.

Jonathan Edwards writes of Lucifer: 'But when it was revealed to him, high and glorious as he was, that he must be a ministering spirit to the race of mankind which he had seen newly created, which appeared so feeble, mean, and despicable, so vastly inferior, not only to him, the prince of the angels, and head of the created universe, but also to the inferior angels, and that he must be subject to one of that race that should hereafter be born, he could not bear it. This occasioned his fall...'[3]

While we cannot pronounce on the precise set of circumstances at the time of Lucifer's sin, we do know that the essence of it was pride (1 Timothy 3:6). Is it any wonder that this sin is so very hateful to God? It was the first sin, and it is the root of every other sin.

We also know that Lucifer was joined in his sin by one third of the original angels (Revelation 12:4).

The fallen Lucifer

Needless to say, this ill-conceived rebellion did not succeed. It resulted in Lucifer and the rebellious angels being cast out of heaven (Isaiah 14:12). The book of Revelation describes this rebellion in this way: 'And war broke out in heaven: Michael and his angels fought with the dragon; and the dragon and his angels fought, but they did not prevail, nor was a place found for them in heaven any longer. So the great dragon was cast out, that serpent of old, called the Devil and Satan, who deceives the whole world; he was cast to the earth, and his angels were cast out with him' (Revelation 12:7-9).

After his fall from heaven, Satan does not appear again in Scripture until after God created Adam and Eve and placed them in the Garden of Eden. There he succeeded in causing Adam and Eve to rebel against God (Genesis 3). This is the reason Ezekiel says:

> 'You were in Eden, the garden of God'
>
> (28:13).

This statement alone is sufficient to show us that this passage must not be applied to the king of Tyre alone.

The final result of Lucifer's rebellion is yet to come, namely, that moment when Satan is finally cast into the lake of fire (Revelation 20:10).

The rebellion and fall of Lucifer raise difficult and piercing questions. Why did God not prevent Lucifer from rebelling? After choosing to allow him to rebel, why did God not

> Each instance of conversion is nothing less than God invading Satan's realm, enlightening the sinner.

21

immediately consign him to the lake of fire? In other words, why did God allow the fallen Lucifer to enter upon his career as Satan the adversary who opposes and resists the work and the rule of God?

We will never be able to satisfactorily answer in this life all the questions that come to mind about God and his ways. We must be content to see part of the truth and to believe that all the truth will finally be revealed. Furthermore, we must believe that when that truth is revealed, it will make perfect sense.

Lessons from Lucifer

While we wait for that time, we must focus on the things which we do know:

1. God is not responsible for evil in the universe. Lucifer was created as a good angel. Evil sprang, not from the heart of God, but from the heart of Lucifer.

2. Satan is a real being who is unceasingly at work in this world to oppose the things of God. He is now focusing his efforts on two points: hindering the spread of the gospel and hindering the progress of those who have received the gospel.

3. Satan is assisted in his efforts by an empire of evil beings. He is the head of principalities, powers, the rulers of the darkness of this age and spiritual hosts of wickedness in the heavenly places (Ephesians 6:12).

4. Satan primarily depends on subtlety or deceitfulness to advance his work (2 Corinthians 11:3, 13-15). This is the reason the apostle Paul warns us to stand 'against the wiles of the devil' (Ephesians 6:11).

5. God is greater than Satan. He defeated him when he first rebelled. He defeated him again when Jesus died on the cross (Colossians 2:15). And he will defeat him again at the end of human history (Revelation 20:10).

6. God has also decisively defeated Satan in each and every instance of conversion. Every child of God was once Satan's captive and was blinded by him (2 Corinthians 4:3-4). Each instance of conversion is nothing less than God invading Satan's realm, enlightening the sinner (2 Corinthians 4:6) and releasing one of his captives. The apostle John writes: 'We know that we are of God, and the whole world lies under the sway of the wicked one. And we know that the Son of God has come and has given us an understanding, that we may know him who is true; and we are in him who is true, in his Son Jesus Christ. This is the true God and eternal life' (1 John 5:19-20).

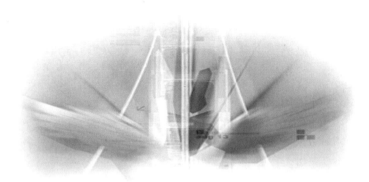

3. At war with Satan

Please read: Ephesians 6:10-20

The being we know as Satan was created as Lucifer. He was supreme among the angels until he rebelled against God (Isaiah 14:12-17). As we have noted previously, that rebellion led to him being cast out of heaven along with all those angels who joined forces with him.

Since that time, Satan has tirelessly pursued a career of opposing God. Because he is opposed to God he is opposed to the people of God. This means, among other things, that the people of God are in a war against Satan and his armies.

The nature of this war

Paul's words to the Ephesians indicate something of the nature of the warfare Satan conducts against God's people. First, he often resorts to 'wiles' in this warfare. He can roar like the lion (1 Peter 5:8), but generally he prefers to rely on his ability to deceive. So effective is he at this point that the apostle Paul found it necessary to say repeatedly to his churches, 'Do not be deceived' (1 Corinthians 3:18; 15:33; Galatians 6:7; Ephesians 5:6; 2 Thessalonians 2:3; James 1:22; 1 John 1:8; 3:7).

Paul also mentions 'principalities and powers'. This phrase seems to indicate the power and authority attained by those angels who joined Satan in his rebellion. His reference to 'rulers of the darkness of this age' indicates that the spiritual and moral darkness of this world must be explained in terms of the control that these satanic forces exert.

When referring to 'spiritual hosts of wickedness' Paul presents us with the number and nature of the satanic forces. A host is a significant number, but these forces consist of many 'hosts'. And they are totally devoted to evil. John Eadie says their 'appetite for evil only exceeds their capability for producing it'.[1]

Satan is never happier than when people believe he does not exist.

In addition to all these details, Paul tells us these forces are 'in the heavenly places', which is evidently his way of emphasizing the superhuman nature of these evil spirits.

Later in his description, Paul refers to Satan's 'fiery darts' (Ephesians 6:16). These may very well refer to sudden, fierce attacks of Satan. They may come in the form of blasphemous thoughts, doubts, or evil imaginations that suddenly crop up in the mind and seem to stick there.

Many people scoff at such details and, in doing so, fall into one of the wiles of the devil. He is never happier than when people believe he does not exist. But exist he does, and consequently the church is engaged in fierce warfare every day of her existence in this world.

One of the primary weapons Satan wields in his warfare against the church is false teaching. The apostle Paul was keenly aware of this weapon and constantly warned his churches regarding it. He cautioned the Corinthians about Satan's ability to 'transform himself into an angel of light' and the ability of his ministers to transform themselves into 'ministers of righteousness' (2 Corinthians 11:14-15). As he was taking his leave of the Ephesian elders, he put them on notice that 'savage wolves' would come among them who would not 'spare the flock', but would rather speak 'perverse things' (Acts 20:29-30).

He also warned the Christians in Philippi of 'enemies of the cross of Christ' (Philippians 3:18). Again and again the apostle sounded the alarm. He called his young ministers, Timothy and Titus, to be ever watchful against false teachers (1 Timothy 1:3-7, 18-20; 4:1-5; 6:3-11; 2 Timothy 1:15; 2:17-18; 3:6-9, 13; Titus 1:10-16) and to make sure that they subscribed to sound doctrine (1 Timothy 1:10; 2 Timothy 4:3; Titus 1:9; 2:1).

It is very important for us to realize that Paul was not alone in this emphasis. The authors of Hebrews, Peter, John and Jude sounded the alarm as well (Hebrews 13:9; 2 Peter 2:1-3, 14-19; 1 John 4:3; 2 John 7-11; Jude 4, 11).

We must not leave the warfare that Satan conducts against the church without calling attention to its focal point. There is nothing Satan hates more than the cross of Christ. That cross

27

> The cross trumpets the truths of God's holiness, man's sin, and the blood atonement, and Satan fiercely hates each of them.

declares truths he simply cannot tolerate. It proclaims that man is a sinner; that his sin is a very serious matter, so serious that it deserves the condemnation of hell; that man can do nothing about his own sin. But, thank God, that cross also triumphantly announces that God has in and through the shed blood of his Son exercised his judgement on the sins of his people, and there is, therefore, no condemnation left for them.

That cross trumpets the truths of God's holiness, man's sin, and the blood atonement, and Satan fiercely hates each of them. He, therefore, works feverishly to send out into this world false teachers who are 'enemies of the cross of Christ' (Philippians 3:18), to corrupt minds from 'the simplicity that is in Christ' (2 Corinthians 11:3) and to declare 'another Jesus' (2 Corinthians 11:4). Such teachers are very troubling because they 'pervert' the gospel of Christ (Galatians 1:7).

The resources for this war

It may be intimidating to read about the malevolent designs of Satan and the subtlety and ferocity with which he attacks the church. We may read some of these details and find ourselves wondering how the church can ever hope to survive in such a war. Scripture holds before us several truths to encourage and comfort us.

The church has been given an armour

The apostle refers to this armour as 'the armour of God' (Ephesians 6:11). It is God who provides it. If the church were to seek to fight in her own strength, she would most certainly fail, but in God's armour she succeeds.

The following parts of the armour are those that may be considered to be defensive in nature.

The girdle of truth (v. 14). Before she can ever hope to resist Satan, the church must be settled in her convictions. She must rest in confidence that she has the truth that was 'once for all delivered to the saints' (Jude 3). There is no hope for success in spiritual warfare if the church believes that truth is never certain and ever changing.

The breastplate of righteousness (v. 14). The central tenet of the gospel is that guilty sinners can stand in the presence of the holy God by being clothed in the perfect righteousness of the Lord Jesus Christ. The imputed righteousness of Christ leads to an imparted righteousness. Because God's people are sanctified by the Spirit of God, they seek to practise righteousness. One of the ways Satan attacks the church is by sowing seeds of doubt. Those who make up the church can withstand the onslaught of doubt by pointing Satan to the perfect righteousness of the Lord Jesus Christ.

29

The feet shod with the preparation of the gospel of peace (v. 15). The soldier's shoe gave firmness of footing and readiness to move forward. The peace created by the gospel — peace with God, peace with others, and peace within — enables the people of God to stand against the anxieties Satan hurls their way. That same peace gives the children of God an eagerness to share the gospel with others.

The shield of faith (v. 16). This shield is given by God to enable his people to quench Satan's 'fiery darts', that is, any sudden attack from Satan that causes wicked, ungodly thoughts or worries to fix themselves in the mind. The Christian wields the shield of faith to counter such attacks by pointing Satan to the complete adequacy of the Lord Jesus Christ and by relying on the revealed character of God and his promises.

The helmet of salvation (v. 17). In his first letter to the Thessalonians, the apostle Paul designates this helmet as 'the hope of salvation' (1 Thessalonians 5:8). Satan loves to discourage the church by suggesting that she is engaged in a hopeless, futile enterprise. Believers take up the helmet of salvation when they fortify their minds with the promises of God regarding the future. Those promises assure us that the Lord Jesus Christ will return to take his people home and they will then be finally and completely vindicated.

The church has been given a weapon

After listing the defensive parts of the armour Paul proceeds to call attention to the weapon the church is given, namely, 'the sword of the Spirit, which is the word of God' (Ephesians 6:17).

The Word of God has both a defensive and offensive aspect. By relying on its teaching, the people of God can fend off Satan's attack. By wielding it in proclamation, they can put him and his forces to flight.

The classic example of this is, of course, Satan's temptation of the Lord Jesus Christ in the wilderness. Three times Satan tempted Jesus and each time our Lord responded by saying: 'It is written...' (Matthew 4:4).

The Word of God is a very powerful and potent weapon because it is 'living and powerful, and sharper than any two-edged sword' (Hebrews 4:12).

As the church employs this her powerful weapon, she will see Satan's 'strongholds', that is, his fortifications, pulled down. And the arguments Satan plants in sinners, arguments that they use to exalt themselves against the knowledge of God, will be cast down. Through the power of the Word of God, the church can expect to see such sinners captured and brought into obedience of Christ (2 Corinthians 10:4-5).

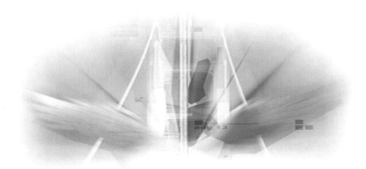

4. What the cherubim have to say

Please read: Ezekiel 1:4-28

The prophet Ezekiel saw the cherubim in a vision by the River Chebar (vv. 1-3). We know that the creatures he saw were cherubim because he later says: 'And the cherubim were lifted up. This was the living creature I saw by the River Chebar' (10:15).

Each one had four faces and four wings (v. 6). One of their faces was that of a man; another was that of a lion; a third was that of an ox; and the fourth was that of an eagle (v. 10). Some interpreters take the faces to represent respectively the intelligence, strength, faithful service and swiftness of the cherubim.

Furthermore, the legs of the cherubim were straight, and their feet were 'like the soles of calves' feet' (v. 7). They had 'the hands of a man under their wings' (v. 8). Ezekiel also tells us that their colour was like that of 'burnished bronze (v. 7).

The cherubim seem to have a special connection with the holy presence of God and the throne of God. However, in this particular chapter we are interested in their testimony to us, that is, in what they have to say to us, although it is a bit misleading to put it in that way. The truth is that the cherubim never speak in Scripture. However, they *do* speak by their mere presence.

If we could propel ourselves through time and interview Ezekiel, we would certainly find him affirming that the cherubim had definitely delivered a message to him. By appearing to him in this vision, the cherubim declared to him and to his fellow Israelites certain truths that they urgently needed. These are truths that we need as much as they did, and apply as much to us as they did to them.

We will now look at three of these truths.

Don't ever think that God has deserted you

Before we can appreciate this truth, we must get our bearings. Ezekiel was a prophet to the people of Judah during their years of captivity in Babylon. This captivity came about in three stages.

- In 605 B.C. when Daniel and his friends were taken.
- In 597 B.C. when ten thousand more of Judah's citizens, including Ezekiel, were taken.
- In 586 B.C. when Nebuchadnezzar and his forces dealt the final blow to Judah by destroying the city of Jerusalem and carrying away even more captives.

34

Ezekiel seems to have begun his prophetic ministry around 592 B.C. and continued it until the year 570. It was there in Babylon that Ezekiel received this vision of the cherubim. What did this mean?

Many of the Jews had a tendency to believe that God was present only in the temple. On the basis of this vision, Ezekiel could assure his fellow captives that God was present there in Babylon just as he was in the temple of Jerusalem.

◇◇◇◇◇◇◇◇◇◇◇◇◇◇◇◇◇◇◇◇

God never abandons his people. He is present with them even in their trials.

◇◇◇◇◇◇◇◇◇◇◇◇◇◇◇◇◇◇◇◇

Our circumstances can be such that we can also be tempted to believe that God has abandoned us. It is not true! God never abandons his people. He is present with them even in their trials.

Don't ever think that God has lost control or failed in his purpose

We draw this conclusion from the wheels with which the cherubim were associated. The prophet writes: 'Now as I looked at the living creatures, behold, a wheel was on the earth beside each living creature with its four faces' (Ezekiel 1:15).

But Ezekiel saw more than just wheels. He says, 'The appearance of their workings was, as it were, a wheel in the middle of a wheel' (v. 16). We are evidently to understand each wheel being, in the words of Derek Thomas, 'intersected by another, probably at right angles'.[1]

So now we have wheels inside of wheels. What does all this suggest? The wheels deal with life in this world. They were 'on the earth' (v. 15).

Furthermore, the wheels depict the complexity and difficulty of life in this world. There are wheels within wheels! Do we not have here a very fitting and apt picture of life on this earth? Constant change and incredible complexity! Life is so very much like this that it often seems to us to make no sense at all. How thankful we should be that Ezekiel saw more than wheels!

What else did he see? First, he noticed the particular and precise way in which these wheels moved, that is, going in any one of four directions without turning (v. 17). The fact that the wheels could go in any one of four directions tells us that God's providence manifests itself in all parts of the earth. No part is excluded. The fact that the wheels go in these directions without turning tells us that God's purposes are never defeated or thwarted. He never has to reverse his course or change his plans.

To understand this part of Ezekiel's vision, we only have to think of our own attempts to carry out our plans. We strike off in one direction only to encounter difficulty. We then have to go back or change direction. But God never runs into unforeseen difficulties. He never has to abandon his plans or to change direction. He is never surprised or caught off guard.

Secondly, he noticed that these wheels were full of eyes (v. 18). The eyes speak of intelligence and discernment. The wheels which Ezekiel saw were moving, then, in conjunction with the wisdom of God. They were not moving arbitrarily, without rhyme or reason.

Finally, he noticed that these wheels always followed the living creatures (vv. 19-21). In other words, they follow the cherubim, who represent God. The wheels, therefore, follow God. The way our circumstances move is the way that God moves. This is because God is in all our circumstances.

All of this had tremendous value for Ezekiel and his fellow captives. Their circumstances were such that it looked as if things were running out of control. We might say their circumstances were such that it looked as if the wheels of life were turning aimlessly in first one direction then another without any apparent purpose at all.

Through the vision of the cherubim God delivered to Ezekiel the calming message that such impressions were mistaken. Their circumstances were being controlled by the God of perfect intelligence. Their circumstances were moving in the very direction which he had planned. And nothing would cause him to deviate from the purposes which he had in mind for them.

The same is, of course, true of us. God is at work in all circumstances for our good and according to his purposes (Romans 8:28). No truth is harder for us to believe. And many Christians confess that they have a very hard time accepting it. Like Job of old, they want God to give them the explanation for all their difficulties. Then they will trust him! But God calls us to trust him now and promises to give the explanation later.

We would all do well to remember this part of Ezekiel's vision — the rims of the wheels 'were so high they were awesome' (v. 18). God's wise purposes are much higher than we will ever be able to comprehend in this life. When God finally makes them plain to us, we will join Job in saying to God:

'I know that you can do everything,
And that no purpose of yours can be withheld from you.
...I have uttered what I did not understand,
Things too wonderful for me, which I did not know'

(Job 42:2-3).

Don't ever think that anyone is greater than God

The majesty of God is everywhere in this vision. The cherubim, impressive as they were, could not begin to compare with God. This is drilled home by Ezekiel's use of the words 'above' and 'over' (vv. 22, 25, 26). Ezekiel and his fellow captives must have realized that the God who was greater than the cherubim must most certainly be greater than King Nebuchadnezzar!

How much greater is God than the cherubim? Over the cherubim was a 'firmament' or expanse (v. 22), and God was above the expanse (v. 25). The cherubim themselves were in no doubt about the superiority of God, letting down their wings at the sound of his voice (v. 25).

The majesty of God was also depicted by the expanse gleaming like an 'awesome crystal' (v. 22), the sound of his voice (v. 25), the appearance of his throne, which was 'like a sapphire stone' (v. 26), and the shimmering of a rainbow (v. 28).

High above the throne 'was a likeness with the appearance of a man' (v. 26), who was clothed in brightness (v. 27). Who was this man? It can be none other than an Old Testament picture of the Lord Jesus Christ himself. Here is the gist of it — God in his majesty has determined that Jesus Christ should have pre-eminence in all things (Colossians 1:18).

The only way for us to know the majestic God is through faith in the redeeming work of Jesus Christ. And we can never trust in Jesus if we insist on putting angels above him. The cherubim remind us that they themselves worship him. If we want to please the cherubim, we must do the same.

5. Key appearances of the cherubim

Please read: Genesis 3:24; Exodus 37:1-9

The cherubim constitute one of the various types of angels that God created. The passages before us are pivotal in coming to a true understanding of this type of angel.

As we have already noted, the cherubim never deliver a message directly from God to human beings. They seem to have a special connection with the holy presence of God and with the throne of God.

The cherubim at the gate of Eden

While the cherubim never utter any words in Scripture, their mere presence speaks volumes. The first time we encounter them is at the Garden of Eden. After God drove Adam and Eve out of the garden, 'He placed cherubim at the east of the garden of Eden, and a flaming sword which turned every way, to guard the way to the tree of life' (Genesis 3:24).

God could have closed access to the Garden of Eden in any one of several ways. Why did he choose this particular way? There is no difficulty here. By stationing the cherubim at the entrance of the garden, the Lord was pointedly declaring the truth that sinful men and women can never regain paradise until the holy demands of God are satisfied on their behalf.

Do we understand this? Paradise represents fellowship with God, and sin ruins that fellowship. We see this in the case of Adam and Eve. Before disobeying God, they had enjoyed fellowship and communion with him. But after they disobeyed, that fellowship was disrupted (Genesis 3:8-10).

What is necessary for that fellowship to be renewed or restored? To sinful men and women, it is all so very simple. It is merely a matter of God ignoring our sin. But the cherubim remind us that God is holy. Because he is holy, he cannot ignore sin. His holy character demands that the penalty of sin be paid. And that penalty is nothing less than death in all its forms (Romans 6:23).

Throughout the centuries, men have resisted this teaching. Some have argued that there is no paradise to enter, that there is no such thing as fellowship with God in this life and certainly no fellowship with him in heaven. They contend that the only paradise available to man is the paradise that he himself can create in this world through social reform, government, education and culture.

So far the results are not encouraging. After many, many years of trying, there is no indication that man is any closer to creating a paradise on this earth. War, crime, ignorance, corruption and a thousand other paradise-wreckers flow on unabated.

Yet the paradise-creators remain undaunted. It is only a matter of more time, more effort, more programmes, more money, and paradise will finally come. Meanwhile the cherubim continue their unrelenting watch at the gate of Eden saying: 'No paradise until we are satisfied.'

Others have suggested that there is indeed such a thing as fellowship with God in this life and in the life to come. There are cherubim that must

Paradise represents fellowship with God, and sin ruins that fellowship.

be satisfied, and this can be achieved by doing good works and taking part in religious activities. The belief in salvation by works is as old as the human race. But the cherubim remain unimpressed.

How, then, can the cherubim be satisfied? More to the point, how can the holy God they represent be satisfied?

God himself gave the answer to Adam and Eve there in Eden when he killed animals and used their skins to cover Adam and Eve (Genesis 3:21). Those animals had no intrinsic value or worth. There was nothing about their death that could take away Adam and Eve's sin. The significance of their deaths lay in what they pictured. Those animals pointed Adam and Eve ahead to the coming of one whose death would have tremendous value — the Lord Jesus Christ himself.

Here we come to the very heart and core of the Christian message. Before sinners can ever re-enter paradise — fellowship with God — the penalty of sin has to be paid. Sinners have to pay it themselves or someone has to pay it for them.

In all of human history, there is only one who can receive the penalty of sin for others, and that is the Lord Jesus. He, the second person of the Trinity, took our humanity. This is crucial. It was humanity that owed the debt to God, and it was humanity that had to pay. The Lord Jesus had to be one of us to do something for us.

In that humanity, the Lord Jesus lived a sinless life. This is also absolutely vital. If Jesus had committed so much as a single sin, he would have had to pay the penalty for his own sin and could not, therefore, have paid for the sins of anyone else.

In that sinless humanity, he went to the cross to die a death such as no one before or anyone since has died. There on the cross, he received the penalty for sinners. He experienced the wrath of God. He endured an eternity's worth of separation from God in the space of a few hours. That is why he cried: 'My God, my God, why have you forsaken me?' (Matthew 27:46).

Unbelievers often wonder what Christians mean when they speak of being saved by the blood of Christ. The blood represents life being poured out or death; and death is, as we have been noting, the penalty for our sins.

The good news of the Bible is that the Lord Jesus did everything necessary for our sins to be forgiven. He stood in the place of sinners. He took the penalty due to them; and in taking that penalty, he satisfied the holy demands of God. With the cherubim at the gate of Eden, God said that he could not have fellowship with sinners until the penalty of sin was paid. Jesus paid it! Since God demands that the penalty be paid once, there is no penalty left for all those who believe in Jesus to pay!

If you and I want to enter paradise, we must trust ourselves completely to the saving work of Jesus. We must renounce all other hopes, and rest ourselves on what he did on the cross.

The cherubim above the mercy seat

The truth of the atoning death of Christ is driven home again by the cherubim in their next appearance in Scripture, namely, hovering over the Ark of the Covenant. This was a box overlaid with gold with a cover of solid gold above it and cherubim on each side with their wings outstretched over the box.

Inside the box were the tables of stone on which God had written the Ten Commandments. This represented God's holy character.

The mercy seat was the place where the blood of atonement was sprinkled by the high priest on the annual Day of Atonement. The fact that the cherubim on the ark looked down at the mercy seat where the blood was sprinkled by the priest takes us to the meaning of the atonement. The cherubim, representing God, did not see the law and its demands because it was inside the box, which was covered by the mercy seat where the blood fell. The blood of the sacrifice sprinkled on the mercy seat indicated that the demand of God's law for the death of the sinner had been satisfied. The blood of the mercy seat covered the demand of the law.

The mercy seat was a glorious anticipation of the death of Jesus on the cross. The apostle Paul says God the Father 'set forth' Christ as a 'propitiation' (Romans 3:25). The Greek word translated 'propitiation' in this verse is translated as 'mercy seat' in Hebrews 9:5. By his death on the cross, the Lord Jesus Christ became our mercy seat. To propitiate means to appease or placate wrath or anger. The good news of the gospel is that God placated his own wrath against his people by pouring it out on his Son as their substitute.

All of this tells us that the cherubim are not cuddly little creatures to help us over life's little bumps. They rather speak to us about the holy majesty of God, the seriousness of human sin and the complete sufficiency of Christ's death. Thank God for the testimony of the cherubim!

6. In the school of the seraphim

Please read: Isaiah 6:1-7; Revelation 4:1-11

The seraphim are another order or type of angels that God created. The word 'seraphim' means 'burning ones'. It is difficult to say what this means. Some say it is a reference to the seraphim being aflame with devotion to God. The problem with that view is that it suggests that other types of angels are less devoted to the Lord. This, of course, is not true. The explanation may be that the appearance of the seraphim is such that they look as if they are on fire.

These glorious beings are mentioned only in the passages before us. Both the prophet Isaiah and the apostle John saw them in visions. While John does not call them by name, his description makes it clear that they were the same beings that Isaiah saw.

As we examine these two passages, certain truths emerge about the seraphim. We will look at three of these.

They are devoted to the worship and the work of God

Both passages tell us that each of the seraphim had six wings. Isaiah goes into more detail. Two wings were used to cover the face, two to cover the feet and two to fly (Isaiah 6:2).

What are we to understand from the seraphim covering their faces?

We shield our faces when we are confronted with something that is especially bright or dazzling. The seraphim undoubtedly covered their faces for the same reason, that is, to shield themselves from the dazzling glory of God who dwells in 'unapproachable light' (1 Timothy 6:16).

The seraphim themselves are glorious creatures. How glorious is God that even the seraphim find it necessary to shield their faces! In other words, the shielding of their faces is an expression of the immense reverence they have for God. We are much farther removed from God than the seraphim. If they reverence God, how much more should we!

What are we to make of them covering their feet?

We know that our feet represent our creatureliness. They connect us with this earth. When Moses encountered God at the burning bush, God commanded him to take the shoes off his feet (Exodus 3:5). He was in the presence of almighty God, and the fitting response was for him to acknowledge his own creatureliness. While the seraphim are not creatures of this earth, they are still creatures. In the presence of the glorious God, they are compelled to acknowledge their limitation.

And what about the flying of the seraphim?

This merely means that they quickly and readily respond to God's commands. We may picture them as hovering around the throne of God. Like hummingbirds, they can at any second dart away in response to God's commands.

David Jeremiah notes that the seraphim have four wings for worship and two for work.[1] While we certainly are to work for the Lord, we must ever give priority to worshipping him. Only through worship can we be truly prepared for the work!

The apostle John adds one detail that Isaiah omits, namely, the seraphim were 'full of eyes around and within' (Revelation 4:8). This detail is probably intended to drive us to the conclusion that the seraphim are constantly and unrelentingly vigilant. They never cease focusing on God. They are ever conscious of him and ever alert to his commands.

> How glorious is God that even the seraphim find it necessary to shield their faces!

The visions of Isaiah and John tell us more about the God of the seraphim than the seraphim themselves. He is glorious beyond measure and worthy of reverence. He is such a God that we must humble ourselves in his presence. He is worthy of our glad and prompt obedience. These visions lead us to note a second feature or aspect of the seraphim.

They declare the holy character of God

Having described how the seraphim appeared, Isaiah proceeds to relate what they said:

'Holy, holy, holy is the Lord of hosts;
The whole earth is full of his glory!'

(Isaiah 6:3).

The apostle John also heard the seraphim repeating the word 'Holy!' We would do well to look upon the seraphim as teachers, to enrol in their school and to give them rapt attention at this point.

There is nothing about God that is more essential for us to know than this: he is holy! This means that he is of such a nature that he cannot be neutral or ambivalent about our sins. His nature is such that he must detest sin and pronounce and execute judgement upon it.

Many have persuaded themselves that God's fundamental attribute is love. If they were to write the script, they would have the seraphim chanting:

'Love, love, love is the Lord of hosts;
The whole earth is full of his love.'

Let us never for one moment doubt the love of God. The Bible flatly affirms that God is love (1 John 4:8). But there is only one time in the Bible in which an attribute of God is given a threefold emphasis, and that attribute is holiness!

We must understand, therefore, that while God is love, he never loves at the expense of his holiness or at the cost of denying his holiness. The love of God itself is a holy love. As great as the love of God for sinners is, let us always be clear on this: God could not pardon sinners out of love, without satisfying his holiness.

This, by the way, is what we see in the death of Jesus on the cross. Yes, a thousand times yes, the love of God was there (John 3:16). But so also was the holiness of God. Where do we see it? In the cry of Jesus, 'My God, my God, why have you forsaken me?' (Matthew 27:46)!

Jesus was forsaken of God because God-forsakenness is what God's holiness demanded as the penalty for our sins.

They reveal the forgiving grace of God

While we must ever insist on the holiness of God, we must never take it to mean that God is not gracious. He is both holy and gracious, and anyone who seeks to persuade us to choose one of these attributes is asking us to separate friends!

After Isaiah received the message of God's holiness, he received the message of his forgiving grace. There in the presence of the holy God, Isaiah realized how very sinful he was and cried:

'Woe is me, for I am undone!
Because I am a man of unclean lips,
And I dwell in the midst of a people of unclean lips;
For my eyes have seen the King,
The LORD of hosts'

(Isaiah 6:5).

R. C. Sproul describes Isaiah's awareness of his sinful condition in this way: 'Isaiah was groveling on the floor. Every nerve fiber in his body was trembling. He was looking for a

51

place to hide, praying that somehow the earth would cover him or the roof of the temple would fall upon him, anything to get him out from under the holy gaze of God. But there was nowhere to hide. He was naked and alone before God … Relentless guilt screamed from his every pore.'[2]

But God did not leave Isaiah in this position. Sproul writes: 'The holy God is also a God of grace. He refused to allow his servant to continue on his belly without comfort. He took immediate steps to cleanse the man and restore his soul.'[3]

What did the Lord do? He sent one of the seraphim to touch Isaiah's lips with a hot coal from the altar. This conveyed to Isaiah that the Lord had indeed cleansed him of his sin.

The God of grace still promises forgiveness to all who will join Isaiah in confession of sin. The apostle John declares: 'If we confess our sins, he is faithful and just to forgive us our sins and to cleanse us from all unrighteousness' (1 John 1:9).

The visions God gave Isaiah and John were not merely to satisfy their curiosity about the seraphim. The visions were rather designed to put these two men in 'the school of the seraphim'. The visions were intended to teach them that God was worthy of their worship and work, that he is awesome in his holiness and graciously forgives sins.

The school of the seraphim is still receiving students. Let us determine that we shall be among them!

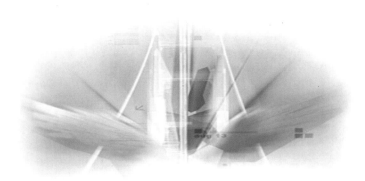

7. Gabriel, God's preaching angel[1]

Please read: Daniel 8:16; 9:20-27; Luke 1:5-20, 26-38

There are many, many angels. Some estimate that their numbers run into billions. Bildad, Job's friend, was not right about everything, but he was surely right in suggesting the vast number of the angels: 'Is there any number to his armies?' (Job 25:3). With so many angels, it is quite impressive that only Gabriel and Michael have their names recorded in Scripture.

The Bible records four appearances of Gabriel (two in Daniel and two in Luke). Because Gabriel revealed truth from God on each of these occasions, he has been called 'God's preaching angel'. The fact that three of Gabriel's appearances dealt with the birth of the Lord Jesus has led some to call him 'God's Christmas angel'.

Gabriel preaches to Daniel (Daniel 8:16; 9:20-27)

Gabriel appeared twice to Daniel in Babylon almost five hundred years before Jesus was born.

The first was to give Daniel understanding of a vision the prophet had. This was the vision of a ram and a goat (8:1-14). The ram represents the Medo-Persian Empire, and its two horns represent the Medes and Persians merging into one. The goat represents Greece and its great horn relates to Alexander. The four horns represent the generals who became kings after Alexander's kingdom was divided into four parts. The little horn represents Antiochus Epiphanes, who rose from the third empire to rule one of these four parts, namely, the Syrian division. Antiochus Epiphanes also represents the final Antichrist.

The second appearance of the angel occurred while Daniel was reading his Scriptures to ascertain exactly when his people's period of captivity in Babylon would come to an end. Suddenly Gabriel appeared and announced that he had come to give him understanding (Daniel 9:2, 22).

Daniel, of course, expected to be given understanding on the matter with which he was occupied, that is, the end of his people's captivity. But Gabriel came to give him insight into a far greater matter, that is, the coming of Christ. In effect Gabriel was sent to Daniel to lift his eyes off the pressing issue of the present (the date of Israel's release from captivity) to matters of far greater importance — the coming of Christ and the purpose for which he would come.

In his message to Daniel, Gabriel said the Messiah would be 'cut off, but not for himself' (Daniel 9:26), that is, he would die but his death would be for others. Through that death he would 'finish the transgression', 'make an end of sins', 'make reconciliation for iniquity', 'bring in everlasting righteousness', 'seal up the vision and prophecy' (fulfill prophecy), and 'anoint the Most Holy' (Daniel 9:24).

Gabriel came to give him insight into a far greater matter, that is, the coming of Christ.

There could be no better statement of the redeeming work of Christ. He died not for himself but for others, and in doing so provided forgiveness for their sins and eternal righteousness before God.

After dying on the cross, the Lord Jesus entered into heaven to make intercession for his people and thus anointed 'the Most Holy'. All of this not only fulfilled the prophecies of Daniel but many other prophecies of the Old Testament as well.

Gabriel preaches to Zacharias (Luke 1:5-20)

On this occasion Gabriel appeared to announce that Zacharias and his wife would soon become the parents of a very special son, John the Baptist. He would play a unique role in God's plan by preparing the way for the Messiah (Luke 1:17). The birth of this special son meant the long-awaited Messiah was, as it were, standing right at the door!

But Zacharias and Elizabeth were well advanced in years. They could not have a child (Luke 1:18)! The thing impossible!

So Zacharias gave way to unbelief, and, as a result, was stricken with a severe judgement, namely, being unable to speak until after John the Baptist was born (Luke 1:20, 23, 63-64). Zacharias reminds us that it is possible to be an unbelieving believer, that is, to actually be a child of God and still refuse to believe the Word of God at one point or another.

It is always tragic to see someone who believes in God and his Word fail to believe at a given point. It is much sadder to see someone never come to faith in God at all. The unbelieving believer robs himself of God's blessings, while the unbeliever robs himself of eternity in heaven with God.

How we need to take all of this to heart! So far as we know Gabriel is not these days appearing to individuals to preach the glorious gospel of Jesus Christ. But that message is still being preached. And with the preaching is the call to believe.

Gabriel preaches to Mary (Luke 1:26-38)

Six months after appearing to Zacharias, Gabriel appeared to Mary to announce the forthcoming birth of the Saviour.

In this appearance, Gabriel stressed the manner of Christ's coming. Christ was to be born like no other. He was to be born of a virgin.

Gabriel explained it to Mary in these words: 'The Holy Spirit will come upon you, and the power of the Highest will overshadow you; therefore, also, that Holy One who is to be born will be called the Son of God' (Luke 1:35). The virgin birth has been much disputed in recent years, but the evidence for it is inescapable.

It is dealt with by two of the Gospel writers, Matthew and Luke. Luke's account of the virgin birth is especially noteworthy because he was a physician and would have been naturally sceptical of a virgin birth. He begins his Gospel by telling us that he had examined carefully the entire gospel story. His words 'having had perfect understanding of all things from the very first' (Luke 1:3) amount to him saying he had 'traced all things accurately'.

In other words, Luke's Gospel is the product of the painstaking research of a man not given to readily accepting myths and superstitions; and yet he gives the fullest account of the virgin birth!

Herschel H. Hobbs writes: 'All of Luke's training and experience would deny the possibility of a virgin birth. To record such an occurrence as a fact would subject him to great criticism. Yet the evidence was so conclusive that he gave the most complete story of the virgin birth of Jesus on record.'[2]

Gabriel's message on the virgin birth emphasized an essential part of the gospel message. There could be no salvation for sinners without it. It is that important! The second person of the Trinity had to take our humanity in order to save us, but he also had to be different from us. If he had not been born of a virgin, he would have been exactly like us and could not, therefore, have done anything for us. In other words, he would have been a sinner himself and in need of redemption.

We must not leave this point without drawing attention to Mary's response. While Zacharias refused to believe Gabriel's message, Mary quickly and readily embraced it even though she had an even greater obstacle to her faith. There was a historical precedent for what Zacharias was being asked to believe, in that Abraham and Sarah had also been told that God would give them a son in their old age (Genesis 18:1-15). There was, however, no precedent for Mary. No virgin had ever conceived and bore a son.

In his appearance to Mary, Gabriel also stressed the duration of Christ's kingdom: 'And he will reign over the house of Jacob for ever, and of his kingdom there will be no end' (Luke 1:33).

Centuries before, God made this promise to King David of Israel: 'I will set up your seed after you, who will come from your body, and I will establish his kingdom… And your house and your kingdom shall be established for ever before you. Your throne shall be established for ever' (2 Samuel 7:12, 16).

That promise was now to be fulfilled. Jesus Christ is the king who reigns for ever, not over an earthly, political kingdom, but rather over a spiritual kingdom. This rule, now in the hearts of his people, will culminate in a kingdom of glory that will be universally acknowledged (Luke 17:21; John 18:36-37; Romans 14:17; Philippians 2:9-11).

What a joy it is to be part of such a kingdom! When other kings and kingdoms have crumbled and passed away, the kingdom of our Lord shall endure!

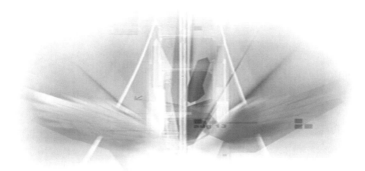

8. Michael, the archangel

Please read: Daniel 10:13, 21; 12:1; 1 Thessalonians 4:16; Jude 9; Revelation 12:7

We have noted that only two angels are actually named in the Bible: Gabriel and Michael. Having examined what the Bible tells us about Gabriel, we now give our attention to Michael the archangel.

The Bible does not explicitly say that Michael is the only angel of this order, but many commentators believe this to be the case. They cite Paul's reference to 'the archangel' (1 Thessalonians 4:16, AV) as an indication that there is only one.

If that is indeed the case, Michael is a very extraordinary being. We might not be too far off the mark if we conclude that he is now supreme among the angels.

The passages which refer to Michael lead us to divide our consideration of him into two parts: his conflict with Satan, and his role at the end of time.

Michael's conflict with Satan (Daniel 10:13, 21; Jude 9; Revelation 12:7)

We first encounter Michael in the book of Daniel in a passage of profound mystery.

Let us first look at the context of the passage. Daniel was by now an old man — eighty-seven, to be precise — and living in Persia, which had conquered Babylon. Daniel had been in this area for a very long time, having been carried captive from Jerusalem by the Babylonians in 605 B.C. As we come upon him now, we find him still hard at work for the Lord, in fasting and prayer (Daniel 10:2-3, 12). This should be a great lesson to us that we are never to retire from that wonderful work!

Suddenly a glorious man appeared (vv. 5-6). Daniel's description of this man is very similar to the apostle John's description of the Lord Jesus Christ in Revelation 1:12-17. This leads us to the conclusion that the man who appeared to Daniel was none other than our Saviour. Stuart Olyott bluntly says: '...Daniel saw the pre-incarnate Lord of glory!'[1]

How did Daniel respond to this vision? Let him answer: '...no strength remained in me; for my vigour was turned to frailty in me, and I retained no strength' (v. 8).

All of this is clear and straightforward. Then in verse 10 we enter the realm of mystery, where Daniel says he was touched by a hand. The one who touched him tells Daniel that he had been delayed in coming for three weeks because 'the prince of the kingdom of Persia' had 'withstood' him (v. 13). It is at this point that Michael enters the picture. The speaker continues: 'Michael, one of the chief princes, came to help me, for I had been left alone there with the kings of Persia' (v. 13).

Adding to the mystery is the speaker's statement that he must 'return to fight with the prince of Persia' and will be again upheld by Michael (vv. 20-21).

Questions abound!

1. Was the person who touched Daniel the Lord whom he had just seen or was it an angel?
2. Who was the prince of Persia?
3. How could this prince detain a heavenly being?
4. What did Michael do to help?
5. Why was all this important for Daniel to know?

Here are my answers:

1. The being who touched Daniel was probably an angel, perhaps even Gabriel (9:21).

2. The prince of Persia is very likely a reference to Satan. Stephen Miller observes: 'Persia ruled the world in that day, and Satan would surely have concentrated his personal efforts in the most influential area.'[2]

It is vital for us to understand that we are dealing here with a crucial juncture in God's plan of redemption, namely, at the very time that Cyrus was deciding whether to release the Jews from captivity. Gleason Archer observes: 'Knowing that such a development could lead to the ultimate appearance of the Son of God as the Messiah for God's redeemed, Satan and all his hosts were determined to thwart the renewal of Israel and the deliverance of its people from destruction.'[3]

3. The Lord could have defeated Satan with a single word and allowed his angel to reach Daniel immediately. Why did he not do so? When an angel is detained, it is because the Lord allows him to be.

What we have here is something very much like the Lord wrestling with Jacob (Genesis 32:22-32). Jacob won the wrestling match because God let him win! By allowing Jacob to win here, God gained victory in other ways!

We have the same principle in the story of Job. God allowed Satan to 'win' with Job so that he, God, could have far more important victories. We shall consider in a moment the Lord's purpose in allowing his message to be delayed.

4. What did Michael do to help? He evidently did the very same thing he had done before, namely, defeat Satan (Jude 9; Revelation 12:7), and in doing so, allow the Lord's messenger to pass.

5. Why was it important for Daniel to know these things? Or, to put it another way, what was the Lord's purpose in allowing Satan to detain his messenger to Daniel?

For three weeks Daniel had been praying and fasting and seeking to understand what the future held for his people (v. 14). Perhaps this information was shared with Daniel to show him that spiritual warfare is real and ever present and that the prayers of God's people play a vital role in it ('I have come because of your words' — v. 12).

It is very easy for us to get caught up in speculation about these matters and lose sight of the truths that are just as important and valid for us as they were for Daniel:

- There is more to this world than meets the eye. Behind what we see are spiritual beings who are engaged in conflict.

- Through their prayers, as we have noted, God's people participate in this spiritual warfare and achieve victories.

- While God allows Satan to have certain leeway, he, God, is greater than Satan and can always defeat him at the time and in the way he chooses (1 John 4:4).

By the way, we can see these same truths displayed when the prophet Elisha was surrounded by the Syrian army (2 Kings 6:8-18).

We have noticed, then, that Michael has been given a special role of combat against Satan. In addition to that, he will evidently fill a special role at the end of time.

> While God allows Satan to have certain leeway, he, God, is greater than Satan and can always defeat him.

Michael's role at the second coming of Jesus (Daniel 12:1; 1 Thessalonians 4:16)

The apostle Paul found it necessary to write to the Thessalonians about the matter of the Lord's coming. Those believers were much confused about the issue and were sorely in need of some clarification.

What wonderful clarification the apostle gave! He wrote to assure them that 'the Lord himself will descend from heaven with a shout'. And the bodies of all believers in Christ will hear that shout and will come out of their graves.

That is not all. Those believers who happen to be living at that time will hear that shout as well. Those believers will be 'caught up ... to meet the Lord in the air'. Living believers will instantaneously be changed from life on earth to life in heaven. They will receive their resurrection bodies without having to pass through the experience of death. What a glorious day of victory that will be!

Paul does not specifically name Michael, but refers rather to 'the voice of an archangel'. It seems likely that the reference is to Michael. Why will he be there? It will not be to lend dignity or majesty to the occasion. The Lord himself will provide enough of that!

Perhaps Michael's presence will serve as part of his reward for serving as 'the great prince' who diligently watches over the people of the Lord (Daniel 12:1).

All of this constitutes very interesting information. Michael must be a most impressive angel. But we miss the point if we allow our gaze to end on him. We must look beyond him to the Lord God who created him, who has used him to defend the people of God and who will again use him when the Lord Jesus returns.

Michael himself would point us to the Lord Jesus Christ. He would especially have us know that we must personally trust the Lord Jesus Christ if we want to share in the glory of that coming resurrection day.

9. The Angel of the Lord

Please read: Genesis 16:7-13; 22:11,15; Exodus 3:1-14; 14:19; 23:20-23; Numbers 22:22-35; Judges 2:1-5; 6:11-12, 20-22; 13:1-23

We have looked at the two angels whose names are given in the Bible — Gabriel and Michael. Now we turn our attention to another special angel. No name is given to him; he is only called the 'Angel of the Lord'.

The passages above make it clear that this is no run-of-the-mill angel. So what do we have here in the passages that mention the Angel of the Lord? I do not hesitate to say that he is none other than the Lord Jesus Christ himself. In other words, each time the Angel of the Lord appears, it is a pre-incarnate appearance of the Lord Jesus, or an appearance of Jesus before he came in human flesh at Bethlehem.

John Calvin writes of the Lord Jesus: 'For even though he was not yet clothed with flesh, he came down, so to speak, as an intermediary, in order to approach believers more intimately.'[1]

This is the reason why many Bibles use a capital letter for the word 'Angel', indicating that this is no ordinary angel.

There are substantial reasons for adopting this view. The first is that the Angel of the Lord identified himself as God on more than one occasion (Genesis 22:15-16; Exodus 3:2, 6).

Secondly, some of those to whom the Angel of the Lord appeared identified him as God (Judges 6:22; 13:21-22).

Then, thirdly, the attributes that belong to God are sometimes ascribed to this Angel. If he possesses the attributes of God, he must be God! On one occasion he was said to be able to forgive sins, which is the prerogative of God alone (Exodus 23:20-21). At the burning bush, he receives worship from Moses (Exodus 3:5), which, again, belongs to God alone.

But what truths are we to glean from these appearances of the Angel of the Lord? That is the central issue. These appearances are not recorded merely to fan our curiosity. As is the case with every part of the Bible, they are written for our spiritual benefit and advancement.

There are several answers to that question. We will here deal with three of them.

The centrality of the Lord Jesus and his redeeming work

In the eternal councils of God, before human history began, the three persons of God entered into covenant with each other on the matter of salvation for sinners.

Then and there it was determined that the second person of the Trinity, the Son of God, would take unto himself human flesh and would in that flesh live righteously and die in the place of sinners, receiving the wrath for their sins. And then and there it was determined that a special honour and glory would be given to the Son for undertaking this work (Philippians 2:9-11; Colossians 1:15-20; Revelation 5:8-14).

After Adam and Eve fell into sin, God came into the Garden of Eden to announce the coming of his Son to provide redemption. From Genesis 3:15 forward, the Old Testament anticipates the coming of the Lord Jesus Christ.

Finally, he came! The eternal God 'became flesh and dwelt among us' (John 1:14). He lived that perfect life (1 John 3:5), and he went to Calvary's cross to receive the wrath of God. When the last drop of that cup had been consumed, he cried out 'It is finished!' (John 19:30). And it *was* finished. There was nothing more to be done for redemption to be provided.

The whole Bible is about this redeeming work. The Old Testament looks forward to it and the New Testament either reports it or looks backward to it. The theme of the Bible is the Lord Jesus Christ. It is about mankind losing his paradise through sin and receiving it again through Christ. It is about man being barred from the tree of life through sin (Genesis 3:24) and being given access to it through Christ (Revelation 22:1-2).

It is not surprising, therefore, that we should find the Lord Jesus Christ making pre-incarnate appearances during the Old Testament through which additional honour was placed upon him for the redeeming work that he would come to accomplish and through which faith in his coming was heightened.

God's knowledge of an involvement in his world

God is not an absentee landlord. He did not create the world only to walk away from it and leave it to itself. He has perfect knowledge of everything and everyone in this world. And when it suits his purposes, he can and does step in. Every miracle is an example of God doing this. And so is every appearance of an angel.

What does all this have to do with us? For one thing, it reminds us that we live before the all-seeing God. Nothing, including even our innermost thoughts and motives, is hidden from his eyes.

It also reminds us that the God who has the power to intervene in the events of this world certainly has the power to bring this world to the end that he has appointed. Sometimes it appears as if the world is a driverless car careening through the night. But this is not the case. God is in control.

The Old Testament appearances of the Angel of the Lord also show us something of the glory and magnificence of God and the proper way to respond to him. If you go through the accounts of those who encountered the Angel of the Lord, you will see how they reacted. Was it with an air of familiarity and 'chumminess'? We know the answer. There was invariably a sense of awe and reverence. There was even a trembling. That was certainly the case with

> The Old Testament appearances of the Angel of the Lord also show us something of the glory and magnificence of God.

Joshua who encountered the 'Commander of the army of the LORD' (Joshua 5:14), who most surely must be regarded as the Angel of the Lord. It was also the case with Gideon (Judges 6:22) and with Manoah and his wife (Judges 13:22).

The church today has a lot of business awaiting her on many issues, but there is no more pressing and urgent business before her than this — to get rid of her chummy familiarity with God and to show him proper reverence and awe.

We have mistakenly assumed that we can make God more attractive to people by casting him as everybody's 'big buddy in the sky'. But all we have done is to convince people that they do not need him. A little God does not inspire worship, service, obedience or trust. And he certainly does not make them tremble, which is exactly what sinners need to be doing.

The reality of divine judgement

While the aspect of judgement is on display in more than one of the appearances of the Angel of the Lord (Numbers 22:22-35; Judges 2:1-5), it is no more plainly stated than in these words from Exodus 23:21: 'Beware of him and obey his voice; do not provoke him, for he will not pardon your transgressions; for my name is in him.' These words were spoken by God about the Angel of the Lord (Exodus 23:20). This same Angel, who had been sent to guide them and bless them (Exodus 23:20), could also bring judgement upon them.

This truth has as much application and relevance for us as it did in the Old Testament. The very same Lord who freely pardons sin will, if provoked, bring judgement. The Lord Jesus himself stressed the judgemental aspect of his work in these words: 'For as the Father has life in himself, so he has granted the Son to have life in himself, and has given him authority to execute judgement also, because he is the Son of Man. Do not marvel at this; for the hour is coming in which all who are in the graves will hear his voice and come forth — those who have done good, to the resurrection of life, and those who have done evil, to the resurrection of condemnation' (John 5:26-29).

John the Baptist made this same point when he spoke these words about the Lord Jesus: 'His winnowing fan is in his hand, and he will thoroughly clean out his threshing floor, and gather his wheat into the barn; but he will burn up the chaff with unquenchable fire' (Matthew 3:12). The pardoning Christ will prove to be the judging Christ for all those who reject his pardon!

The option ever before the sinner is to either fall on this Christ in true repentance, receiving his gift of eternal life, or having that same Christ fall on him in crushing, devastating judgement (Matthew 21:44). Believe on him or beware of him!

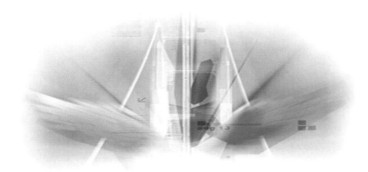

10. Jesus, lower than the angels

Please read: Hebrews 2:5-9

The author of Hebrews must have been a pastor. He wrote as one who was deeply concerned about the spiritual well-being of those to whom he wrote.

His readers were Jewish people who had turned from Judaism to embrace Jesus of Nazareth as the Messiah and the only Lord and Saviour. These people soon began to encounter opposition from family members and friends (10:32-33). They were now wondering if they had been mistaken to break with Judaism, and some of them were thinking about returning to their former beliefs.

The author of Hebrews wrote to persuade them to stay their course. If they were to do so, they must be utterly convinced that Jesus was in every way superior to Judaism. So the author took up his pen in order to demonstrate the superiority of Christ. He did this by showing how those persons and things most venerated by Judaism paled in comparison to Christ. Moses, the priesthood, and the temple itself cannot begin to compare with the Lord Jesus.

The angels were among those most venerated by the Jews, so much so that the author begins his presentation of the superiority of Christ by showing how he far surpasses the very angels themselves (1:1-14).

But the author does something quite surprising. Having argued that Jesus is superior to the angels, he now asserts that Jesus is lower than the angels. It really is an astonishing thought. How often we read words without really thinking about them! Jesus lower than the angels! What an incredible statement!

Ponder it for a moment. The Lord Jesus is the second person of the Trinity. He is God. He is the sovereign Lord of the universe. He is the Creator of all things, and that, of course, includes the angels.

We are confronted then with a puzzle — how can the Christ who is higher than the angels be lower than the angels? Which is it? Is he higher or lower?

To understand the author's point, we must look at three things.

Man as God made him

The author takes his readers back to the creation of mankind. Quoting from Psalm 8:4-6, he reminds them that God made man 'a little lower than the angels' (v. 7).

Although man was made lower than the angels, God had a special purpose for him. We might say that God bestowed a special honour on man. That honour consisted of being set over the world. The point of Psalm 8, which the author of Hebrews is quoting, is to marvel that God would do this for a creature who was made from the dust of the earth. It really is quite amazing!

And there is still more. In addition to granting man dominion over this world, God planned to give him dominion over 'the world to come' (v. 5).

The book of Genesis makes all clear. God put man on this earth with dominion over it. God also put man on trial. After a successful completion of that period of probation, Adam was to be given eternal life or dominion over 'the world to come'. Adam had the opportunity, then, to secure eternal life for all his descendants.

That brings us to the second point.

Man as sin made him

We know how Adam's period of probation turned out. He failed to obey God, and, in doing so, forfeited a great deal of his dominion over this world and also over 'the world to come'.

The author of Hebrews sadly takes notice of this sombre reality in these words about man: 'But now we do not yet see all things put under him' (v. 8). Man had the title to eternal paradise in his hands. But instead of cashing it in and receiving the paradise, he threw it away, as it were. So the story of man is that of an unclaimed paradise. It is the story of a ruined creature. It is the story of a dream smashed to pieces.

Yet, thanks to the grace of God, it is also the story of something else, and that is the redeeming grace of almighty God. Because of this grace, we can also speak of our third point.

Man as God remakes him

We must be absolutely clear on this: God did not have to do anything to redeem sinful man. He could have hung a sign on the door of paradise that read 'Vacant for ever'.

> In our humanity, he went to the cross. There he received the wrath of God in our stead.

But God would not allow Satan and sin to have the final word. The truth is that he had the work of salvation in mind before he ever created the world. That work consisted of the second person of the Trinity stepping into human history to provide salvation.

Here we get to the nub of the matter. Here we discover what the author of Hebrews was saying when he wrote about Jesus being made 'a little lower than the angels' (v. 9). Jesus is the one who made the angels. He is their Lord and Master. He is the object of their praises and their intense and unrelenting devotion.

Why was Jesus made lower than the angels? The answer, of course, is that man was made 'lower than the angels' (v. 7). For Jesus to take our humanity and be one of us, he must of necessity be made 'lower than the angels'. If man is lower, Jesus must be lower as well!

But why was it necessary for Jesus to take our humanity? The answer is in those words which we have used so often — in order to do something for us, he had to be one of us. It was humanity that failed, and it was humanity that must pay the price or penalty for that failure.

It comes down to this: man has to pay the penalty for his sins before he can ever reclaim his paradise. That penalty consists of nothing less than eternal separation from God. Jesus came to pay that penalty on behalf of all those who will believe in him. In our humanity, he went to the cross. There he received the wrath of God in our stead.

Is the penalty for sin separation from God? Jesus cried out from the cross: 'My God, my God, why have you forsaken me?' (Matthew 27:46).

The author of Hebrews tells us that Jesus came to 'taste death' (v. 9). The puritan John Owen explains: '...Christ by tasting of death had experience, knew what was in death, as threatened unto sinners. He found out and understood what bitterness was in that cup wherein it was given him.'[1]

We must be clear on the point I have already made, namely, sin's penalty has to be paid for us before we can ever enter into paradise. But we must be equally clear on another point: God only demands that the penalty for my sin be paid once. If Jesus paid it on my behalf, there is no penalty left for me to pay. It would be unjust of God to allow sinners to enter into paradise without the penalty for their sins being paid. But it would also be unjust of him to demand that I pay the penalty of eternal separation when Jesus has already paid it!

We celebrate nothing less than the gloriously awesome truth that the one who is by nature higher than the angels became lower than the angels. He did so by taking our humanity, and he did that to save sinners. And all who will believe in him will finally be admitted into 'the world to come'.

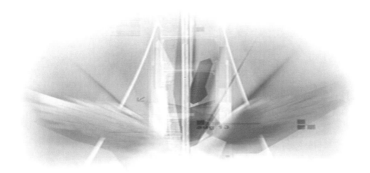

11. Jesus, higher than the angels

Please read: Hebrews 1:1-6

Would you agree with me that angels are very majestic and glorious creatures? The Lord Jesus Christ is much higher!

It is an error of enormous proportions to put angels over the Lord Jesus. The people to whom the author of Hebrews wrote were in danger of doing this very thing. Although they had been converted to Christianity from Judaism, they still retained some of the elements of their former religion. One of these elements was a very high esteem for angels.

The author wasted no time getting to the point. He comes out, as it were, with guns blazing. Jesus is the heir of all things (v. 2). He made all things (v. 2). He is the very 'brightness' of God's glory and the 'express image' of God's person (v. 3). He, Christ, upholds all things by 'the word of his power' (v. 3). Having provided redemption for sinners, he sits at 'the right hand of the Majesty on high' (v. 3).

In order that his readers could not possibly be mistaken about the meaning of all this, the author bluntly says that the Lord Jesus is 'so much better than the angels' (v. 4). How we need this word in this age of angel-mania! Jesus is so much better than the angels!

The author proceeds to support this assertion in terms of what God has *not* said to the angels and what God *has* said to the angels.

What God has not said to any angel (v. 5)

Quoting from Psalm 2:7, the author writes of God: 'For to which of the angels did he ever say:

"You are my Son,
Today I have begotten you?"'

(v. 5).

It is clear that this verse is referring to a very special day. This was the day when the Father spoke to the Son about a special 'begetting', and that act of begetting conferred upon Jesus, the Son of God, a special honour and dignity that no angel can rival. The second person of the Trinity, the Lord Jesus, has always had pre-eminence over the angels, but we are talking here about something that conferred even more dignity and honour on the Son.

What was this act of begetting? When did it take place? The answer is the resurrection of Jesus. In Colossians 1:18, the apostle Paul calls Jesus 'the firstborn from the dead'. And the apostle John does the same in Revelation 1:5 (see also Acts 13:32-33; Romans 1:4; 8:29). Philip Edgcumbe Hughes writes:

> ...the 'day' spoken of here, on which he is said to have been begotten by God, is the day of his glorious victory and vindication, the day also which, for the purposes of our author's argument here, establishes for all to see his absolute superiority to all angels. This 'day' belongs, in the first place, to the event of the resurrection, but it extends also to the ascension of Christ and his glorification at the right hand of the divine majesty. In other words, resurrection, ascension, and glorification should be viewed as forming a unity, each one contributing to the exaltation of the Son to transcendental heights of power and glory.[1]

It was through his resurrection and subsequent ascension that Jesus has 'become so much better than the angels' (Hebrews 1:4).

The Bible tells us that Jesus has always been God. There was never a time when he has not been God. And God is always 'much better than the angels'. So why did the author say Jesus had 'become' better than the angels? Why did he not just say 'Jesus is better than the angels'?

The answer takes us right to the heart of the Christian message. It asserts that the Lord Jesus, the eternal Son of God, for a time became 'lower than the angels' (Hebrews 2:9). As we noted in the last chapter, he did so when he took our humanity. Because human beings are lower than the angels, it was inevitable that Jesus would be lower than the angels when he came in human flesh.

When it appeared as if Jesus was destined to be permanently in this lowly state, astonishingly remarkable and wonderful things happened. He who had become so very low that he died on a Roman cross and was buried in a borrowed tomb sprang from that tomb in glorious resurrection life!

Furthermore, when he arose from the grave, he went from that lowly position to one that was even higher than he had before he came to this earth. This is conveyed by the author's words that Jesus 'has by inheritance obtained a more excellent name' than the angels (v. 4). The apostle Paul puts it like this: 'Therefore God also has highly exalted him and given him the name which is above every name, that at the name of Jesus every knee should bow, of those in heaven, and of those on earth, and of those under the earth, and that every tongue should confess that Jesus Christ is Lord, to the glory of God the Father' (Philippians 2:9-11).

> No angel deserves the honour that the Lord Jesus deserves because no angel has done what he did.

Through his resurrection and ascension, then, the Lord Jesus added to the dignity of his eternal Sonship the dignity and honour of messianic Sonship or, we might say, redeeming Sonship.

The declaration of the Father that Jesus was his Son has to do, not with his eternal Sonship, but with his messianic Sonship. And God the Father has never made that declaration to an angel. It is true that angels are referred to as sons of

God in the book of Job (Job 38:7), but this is in a collective sense. God has never said to any single angel: 'You are my Son.' But he has said that to Jesus Christ, and the fact that he has said it shows the superiority of Christ.

No angel deserves the honour that the Lord Jesus deserves because no angel has done what he did. No angel has taken human flesh, died in the place of sinners, risen from the grave and ascended to the place of honour at the right hand of the Father.

Jesus alone is the Saviour. To bypass Christ, who holds in his hands the gift of salvation, and worship angels is akin to bypassing someone who holds a diamond in his hand in order to receive from another a worthless stone.

What God has said to all the angels (v. 6)

The author of Hebrews shows his readers what God has said to the angels by drawing a quotation from Deuteronomy 32:43:

'Let all the angels of God worship him'

(v. 6).

The author says God spoke these words to the angels 'when he again brings the firstborn into the world'. The word 'again' has caused some to think of the second coming of Christ. That would seem to be the time when God 'again' brings Jesus into this world. But since the previous verses deal with the incarnation, and since the angels obviously worshipped Jesus at that time (Luke 2:14), it is probably correct to translate the phrase: 'And again, when he brings the firstborn into the world...'

In other words, the author is not using the word 'again' to refer to Christ coming again, but rather to an additional argument for the point he is making, that is, the superiority of Christ over the angels. In the words of Geoffrey Wilson, the word 'again' signifies 'the bringing forth of a further proof'.[2]

When did God say this to the angels? The answer is, of course, when Jesus came to this world as a mere babe. At that time, the angels offered adoring worship to him (Luke 2:14).

Now here is the logic of the author of Hebrews: if the angels were commanded to worship the baby Jesus lying in a manger, how much more must they worship the majestic, triumphant Christ who has risen from the dead! And if the angels of God, majestic and magnificent beings that they are, owe worship to the risen and ascended Christ, how much more do we!

Worship is the inevitable response of the mind and heart that have been schooled in the glorious truth of the resurrection. Once we understand the significance of the resurrection, we cannot help but worship the resurrected one.

Let us be assured that the Lord Jesus Christ most certainly arose from the grave. Let us also fix in our minds that special honour has accrued to the Lord Jesus because of his redeeming work. Let us be convinced that no angel deserves the worship that belongs to Christ, and that to honour angels above the Lord Jesus Christ is to insult both the angels and Christ.

So with these things firmly etched in our hearts and minds, let us worship the Lord Jesus in spirit and in truth.

12. Angels as ministering spirits

Please read: Hebrews 1:13-14

The Lord Jesus Christ is higher than the angels. The author of Hebrews abundantly proves this point by powerfully affirming certain truths about Christ (Hebrews 1:1-4). He also proves it in terms of what God has *not* said to angels (vv. 5, 8, 13) and what God has said *to* the angels (v. 6) and *of* the angels (vv. 7, 14).

What has God said *of* the angels? They are ministering spirits (vv. 7, 14). Specifically, they are 'all ministering spirits sent forth to minister for those who will inherit salvation' (v. 14).

These words lead us to raise three questions: to whom do they minister; how do the angels minister to whom they minister; and what does their ministry tell us about God and ourselves?

To whom do the angels minister?

The author of Hebrews leaves no doubt at all about the answer. The angels minister to those 'who will inherit salvation'. The word 'salvation' refers, in the words of Geoffrey Wilson, 'to the future possession of the heavenly inheritance'.[1] It is, of course, one of the grand assumptions of our time that all without exception, or perhaps with very few exceptions, will possess heaven. To suggest otherwise is to declare one's self an ignoramus or, much worse, to commit a hate crime.

Why are Christians willing to risk such things? Why do they insist that all do not have an inheritance in heaven? It is because the Bible steadfastly declares this truth. On one hand, it affirms that only those who trust in the redeeming work of Christ will finally be saved. On the other hand, it just as firmly declares that those who reject Christ will not go to heaven (John 3:16, 18; 3:36; 1 John 5:11-12).

One of the sadnesses of our day is that so many are intensely interested in angels who have no title or right to their ministry! It is an incredible irony that so many are trying to use the angels to bypass Christ while the angels themselves are commissioned to serve only those who know Christ!

The highest priority, then, for those who are interested in angels is to become interested in Christ. Only then will the angels in whom they are interested have interest in them. Most importantly, we need to abandon our sin and receive the Lord Jesus Christ as the only one who can save us from our sins and make us fit for heaven. By the way, the phrase 'who will inherit eternal salvation' raises this question: when are the saved saved? We must answer by saying salvation is past, present and future. Each child of God can say that he has been saved, is being saved and will be saved. He was saved when he received Christ. He is being saved now as the Lord works in his life and matures him. And he will finally be saved when he meets the Lord and is freed from every vestige of sin.

We can now turn to consider the second question raised by our text.

How do the angels minister to the saints?

To put it another way, what are the things that angels do for believers? More precisely, what does God do for his people by sending his angels?

We can summarize their ministry under three headings: through his angels, God guides, strengthens (encourages) and protects or delivers his people.

God guides

This ministry is on display at various points in the Bible. An angel directed Abraham's servant (Genesis 24:7, 40); Philip (Acts 8:26); and Cornelius (Acts 10:3-6).

God strengthens or encourages

This ministry is demonstrated by the experiences of Elijah under the broom tree (1 Kings 19:4-8) and Paul in the midst of a terrible storm at sea (Acts 27:23-24). It is also interesting that God the Father used an angel to strengthen the Lord Jesus himself after his temptations (Matthew 4:11) and in the Garden of Gethsemane (Luke 22:43).

God protects or delivers

This ministry is wonderfully pictured for us by Daniel's safety in the lion's den (Daniel 6:22) and by Simon Peter's escape from Herod's prison (Acts 12:7-11). This particular ministry is affirmed in the following verses:

> 'The angel of the LORD encamps all around those who
>   fear him,
> And delivers them'
>
> (Psalm 34:7).

> '...he shall give his angels charge over you,
> To keep you in all your ways'
>
> (Psalm 91:11).

The angels' ministry of protection prompts us to think about the matter of guardian angels. Many believe that each Christian has been assigned an angel to guard and protect him or her. Those who hold this view do so on the basis of these words from Jesus: 'Take heed that you do not despise one of these little ones, for I say to you that in heaven their angels always see the face of my Father who is in heaven' (Matthew 18:10).

A couple of things must be said about this verse. One is that the term 'little ones' refers to Christians (v. 6) and not merely to children. So the ministry described here, whatever it is, pertains to all the children of God.

Another thing is that this verse does not explicitly say that each Christian has a guardian angel. It rather suggests that the angels are in heaven observing God, who, in turn, is observing his children. With, as it were, a mere glance, God can discharge an angel or any number of angels to assist his people in any way. Those who take the verse to mean each believer has one guardian angel may very well be cheating themselves, as these words from John Calvin indicate:

> **With, as it were, a mere glance, God can discharge an angel or any number of angels to assist his people in any way.**

But whether individual angels have been assigned to individual believers for their protection, I dare not affirm with confidence … We ought to hold as a fact that the care of each one is not the task of one angel only, but all with one consent watch over their salvation … Yet it is not worth-while anxiously to investigate what it does not much concern us to know. For if the fact that all the heavenly host are keeping watch for his safety will not satisfy a man, I do not see what benefit he could derive from knowing that one angel has been given to him as his special guardian.[2]

Before we leave Matthew 18:10, we should note that its major teaching is not so much the guardianship of angels as it is the importance of not despising a child of God. William Hendriksen puts it in these words:

...Jesus is saying to his disciples, 'Do not regard as unimportant those who ... are regarded so highly that he has appointed his most illustrious angels ... to keep watch over them.'[3]

John MacArthur states the same truth:

The fact that Almighty God is so concerned about the care of His beloved children that he has hosts of angels in His presence ready to be dispatched to their aid demonstrates clearly how valuable believers are and how unthinkably wicked it is to look with disdain on someone whom God so highly prizes.[4]

This leaves us one more question to consider.

What does the ministry of angels tell us about God and ourselves?

The ministry of angels yields two crucial conclusions about God. It first tells about God's thorough knowledge of the lives of his people in this world. We sometimes have the impression that he is very distant. The truth is, he is very near. There is not one thing going on the life of any believer of which he is unaware.

It is not enough, of course, to say that God knows about the details of the lives of his people. His heart is involved. He cares for his people. He would not send his angels to minister to them if he did not. But as marvellous as it is to have in the ministry of his angels proof of his care, we have even greater proof of it in the cross of Christ. We need look no farther than the cross to see the heart of God.

What should our response be to such a loving and caring God? Isn't it obvious? We should love him in return! And hearts of love for the God of love will compel us to worship him faithfully, to obey him diligently and to trust him fully. They will also make us desire to be his ministers to others even as the angels themselves are.

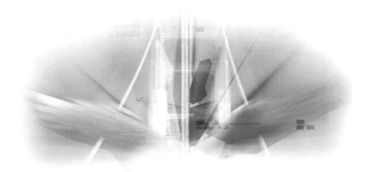

13. Entertaining angels

Please read: Hebrews 13:1-2

As the author of Hebrews moves his letter to a close, he gives his readers a series of crisp commands:

- let brotherly love continue (v. 1)
- do not forget to entertain strangers (v. 2)
- remember prisoners (v. 3)
- let conduct be without covetousness (v. 5)
- remember their leaders (v. 7)
- continually offer praise (v. 15)
- do not forget to do good (v. 16)
- obey leaders (v. 17).

Attached to the second of these is the phrase in which we are interested here: 'some have unwittingly entertained angels' (v. 2). This phrase lends itself to a couple of interpretations, each of which is thrilling and exhilarating.

Entertaining angels who become human

The author of the book of Hebrews urges his readers to 'entertain strangers' (v. 2). He was writing at a time in which travel posed many difficulties for Christian people. The inns were notorious for charging exorbitant fees (and most of the Christians were poor). They were also places in which immorality abounded.

The obvious way for Christians to avoid the inns was, then, to stay with fellow believers. This could only happen if believers were willing to open their homes to travelling Christians, and the author of Hebrews was urging his readers to demonstrate this willingness. To encourage them in this direction, he adds these words: '...for by so doing some have unwittingly entertained angels'.

There can be little doubt that he was thinking of the account in Genesis 18. One day Abraham was sitting 'in the tent door in the heat of the day' (Genesis 18:1). He suddenly saw three men standing nearby and 'ran from the tent door to meet them, and bowed himself to the ground' (18:2). The next few verses record a flurry of activity as Abraham and Sarah bustled about to prepare a meal for their guests (18:3-8).

The long and short of it is that Abraham and Sarah treated these men with warm hospitality only to learn in the process that they were not really men. Their visitors were none other than the Lord himself and two angels in human form. Leaving the Lord with Abraham, the angels then proceeded to Sodom, where they were entertained by Lot (18:16, 22; 19:1-3).

The author of Hebrews explicitly asserts that the very same thing that happened to Abraham, Sarah and Lot could happen with them. In turning away the strangers at their doors, they could be turning away angels!

> **In turning away the strangers at their doors, they could be turning away angels!**

We wish the author had said more. But he tantalizes us with his statement and then moves on. Did he intend to suggest that the saints of every age could expect to entertain angels in human form? Could it be that we ourselves have unknowingly entertained angels? Or was this experience restricted to 'Bible times'?

We can say this is God's world, and he is not shut out of his own world. The God who created this world is always present and at work in it. There is, therefore, nothing to preclude God from sending his angels in human form. We must rest here and wait for eternity to reveal what actually took place in the countless encounters of the average life. In eternity, we may very well find these words from Kent Hughes to be true: 'That tasty hamburger topped with raw onions and served to a hungry stranger may have rested in a celestial stomach — and with no heartburn.'[1]

We have studied angels as ministering spirits (Hebrews 1:14). We must not, therefore, rule out the possibility that angels have ministered to us even when we were totally unaware of it.

We can be sure that the author did not mean for his readers to practise hospitality with an ulterior motive. John MacArthur explains:

We are not to be hospitable because on some occasion we might find ourselves ministering to angels. We are to minister out of brotherly love, for the sake of those we help and for God's glory. The point ... is that we can never know how important and far-reaching a simple act of helpfulness may be.[2]

Entertaining humans who become angelic

That brings us to the second interpretation on this matter of entertaining angels. This view takes the word 'angels' in the generic sense of 'messengers'. It understands 'angels' to refer to human beings and not to heavenly beings. It further maintains that these human beings can at any point serve as God's messengers to us.

We must not let our fondness for the first interpretation cause us to dismiss this one. I maintain that we should not choose between these interpretations but rather embrace both.

We can well imagine something along these lines. Joe Christian has just come home from a long, hard day of work, and Mary Christian is about to set the meal on the table. Suddenly, there is a knock on the door. Joe opens the door and is confronted with the sight of a husband and wife and their two children. The man says: 'I am Bruce Believer, and this is my wife Beth and my children Billy and Belinda. We are Christians, and we have been told that you are as well. We were wondering if you could put us up for the night.' So Joe Christian invites them in, and Mary begins peeling extra potatoes.

After supper, they sit in the living room. By now they have begun to get acquainted and are feeling comfortable with each other. Joe reveals that he and Mary have been carrying a very heavy burden. Some months ago, their only child died very suddenly and unexpectedly. As Joe pours out the grief and heartbreak that he and Mary know, he finds Bruce and Beth Believer are listening with kindness and sympathy. And after the sorrowful tale is told, these two strangers share that they also lost a child. And they begin to talk about how the promises of God had helped them and sustained them. As they speak, Joe and Mary find comfort and consolation.

After Bruce and Beth take their leave the next morning, Joe says to Mary: 'I don't know how you feel, but I cannot help but think that God sent these people our way to give us the message we needed at this time.'

And Mary responds: 'I feel exactly the same way.'

What happened here? Bruce and Beth were not angels, but they became angels. They became God's messengers in that situation, bringing solace to beleaguered and bewildered hearts.

Is it indeed legitimate to understand the word 'angels' in this way? The book of Revelation indicates that it is. The Lord Jesus addressed each of his letters to the churches of Asia Minor with these words: 'And to the angel of the church ... write...' (2:1, 8, 12, 18; 3:1, 7, 14).

It is generally held that the angels of these seven churches were the messengers or pastors. In other words, they were human beings who were called angels. So the author urges his readers to be always ready to entertain their fellow Christians, not only because love itself demanded it (v. 1), but also because it opened the door for blessing. The entertainers never knew when the entertainees would be used by God to deliver a much needed message.

We surely cannot leave this passage without desiring to be 'angels' ourselves. In other words, each believer should make it his business to so master the Word of God and to so cultivate tenderness of heart that he or she can be a source of blessing to his brothers and sisters in the Lord Jesus Christ.

Let's each make it our business to be the type of person that will cause others to think that when they have spent time with us they have been with an angel and not with a devil.

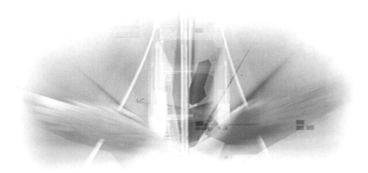

14. Angels desiring to look into salvation[1]

Please read: 1 Peter 1:10-12

The apostle Peter never ceased to be amazed at God's work of salvation. To him it was the most marvellous and glorious thing imaginable. After addressing his readers (vv. 1-2), he immediately launches into a song of praise to God about salvation.

He thanks God for the 'abundant mercy' that has given believers 'a living hope' (v. 3). He rejoices in the 'inheritance' that is 'reserved in heaven' for believers (v. 4). And he freely and gladly acknowledges that all of this is made possible in and through the Lord Jesus Christ (vv. 3, 7).

From this burst of praise for salvation, the apostle proceeds to make it clear to his readers that it fulfilled the prophecies of the Old Testament (vv. 11-12).

This was only one of many evidences that the work of Christ was genuine and could be completely trusted. Specifically, Peter asserts that the prophets of the Old Testament were enabled by 'the Spirit of Christ' (v. 11) to see both 'the sufferings of Christ and the glories that would follow' (v. 11).

Suddenly and unexpectedly Peter brings his discussion of this matter to a close by adding this phrase: 'things which angels desire to look into' (v. 12).

The fact of the angels' interest

The Greek word translated 'look into' is the same word used to describe what Peter himself did when he came to the tomb of the risen Christ. We are told that he stooped down and looked into the tomb (John 20:5). The same word is used of Mary Magdalene when she also looked into the tomb of Christ (John 20:11). By using this word, then, Peter portrays the angels bending over, or, as it were, leaning over the balcony rail of heaven to carefully and intently peer down upon the earth so they can see what God has done and is doing in and through the Lord Jesus Christ.

The Old Testament depicts the very same thing. On top of the Ark of the Covenant was the mercy seat, where the blood of atonement was sprinkled by the high priest. And on each side of that mercy seat was a golden cherub looking down at the very spot where the blood was sprinkled (Exodus 25:18-22).

Cherubim were also depicted on the veil that separated the Most Holy Place from the Holy Place of the tabernacle (Exodus 26:31). The Most Holy Place was that chamber into which the high priest entered once a year to sprinkle the blood on the mercy seat. The depiction of the cherubim on that heavy veil also conveys the desire of the angels to look into salvation through the shedding of blood.

Furthermore, the angel Gabriel was given the responsibility of announcing the forthcoming birth of John the Baptist, Christ's forerunner (Luke 1:11-20), to his father Zacharias, as well as the forthcoming birth of Jesus to his mother Mary (Luke 1:26-33).

A single angel announced the birth of Jesus to shepherds outside Bethlehem (Luke 2:8-12). No sooner were the words out of his mouth than he was joined by 'a multitude of the heavenly host' who burst into praise of God (2:13-14).

> Peter portrays the angels ... leaning over the balcony rail of heaven to ... peer down upon the earth so they can see what God has done and is doing through the Lord Jesus Christ.

The reason for the angels' interest

But why are the angels so interested in the salvation of sinners? We are not surprised to read that the prophets of the Old Testament 'inquired and searched carefully' (1 Peter 1:10) regarding this matter of salvation. We can well understand them desiring to understand better those truths which they were prophesying. But what is this about the angels? Why do they marvel at the mercy of God?

We are out of our element here. Perhaps they study salvation out of amazement that God could love those who had so grievously sinned against him and were, therefore, deserving of nothing but his wrath.

The book of Jude tells us that there were also angels who fell into sin. These 'did not keep their proper domain' because they rebelled against God, but there was no salvation provided for them. They have rather been 'reserved in everlasting chains under darkness for the judgement of the great day...' (Jude 6, see also 2 Peter 2:4).

The fact that there was no salvation offered for the fallen angels must have made salvation for fallen men and women even more amazing to the angels in heaven.

Perhaps the unfallen angels study salvation out of amazement that the Prince of Glory, the eternal Son of God, would stoop so low as to take unto himself the humanity of sinners, and in that humanity would suffer the hostility of sinners and die on a Roman cross.

Perhaps they study salvation out of amazement at the peace and joy of those who have received it. Could it be that there is among the angels a measure of envy (sinless envy, of course) for those of us who have been saved? Do the angels in heaven, who have not sinned and never needed mercy, find themselves wishing that they could experience the joy that such mercy brings? The author of the following lines seemed to think so:

When I sing redemption's story,
The angels will fold their wings;
For angels never knew the joy
That my salvation brings.

There is yet another reason the angels are so keenly interested in salvation. The angels are interested in anything that brings glory to God, and nothing so glorifies God as his wonderful work of salvation. This work displays his grace, his justice and his wisdom in such a way that the angels, who delight in his glory, cannot help but be fascinated by it.

In all likelihood the angels marvel at our salvation for all of these reasons and for reasons that have never even occurred to us.

The challenge of the angels' interest

It is all well and good to know that the angels are interested in salvation, but what does it have to do with us? The fact is, the interest of the angels in our redemption speaks a very powerful word to us.

The angels are God's mighty ones who 'excel in strength' (Psalm 103:20). The angels are God's immortal ones who are beyond the reach of death. The angels are God's faithful ones who ceaselessly and perfectly serve the God who made them (Hebrews 1:7). And they stand in awe of redemption.

If God's mighty, immortal and faithful ones stand in awe of redemption, how much more should those who are weak, dying and sinful. If angels, who have never experienced salvation, are so keenly interested in it, how much greater should be the interest of those who have experienced it!

Is this the case? Is this characteristic of those of us who profess to know the Lord? Are we keenly interested in our Christ and the salvation he has provided? Is it evident to others that this is the main thing in our lives? Is there among us a keen interest in learning more about our salvation? Do we eagerly grab every opportunity to study the Word of God? Do we have a great desire to express gratitude to God for our salvation? Are we anxious to join in public worship and sing praises to his name? Are we eager to do whatever we can to advance his kingdom?

Can we take the following words and truthfully say them to ourselves:

Pause, my soul! adore and wonder!
Ask, 'O why such love to me?'
Grace has put me in the number
Of the Saviour's family;
    Hallelujah!
Thanks, Eternal Love, to thee!

The author of the book of Hebrews saw the Christians to whom he wrote drifting away from the Lord and neglecting their salvation (Hebrews 2:1-4). What would he say if he could observe us for a while? Would his assessment of us be the same as it was of those to whom he wrote? Would he accuse us of neglecting 'so great a salvation'? (Hebrews 2:3).

It is such a great salvation that the angels of heaven themselves are intrigued by it. May God help us to see the greatness of it and to rejoice in it. Let's learn from the angels. Let's allow their interest in salvation to rebuke us for our lack of interest and to renew us in fervent desire to worship and to serve the Lord.

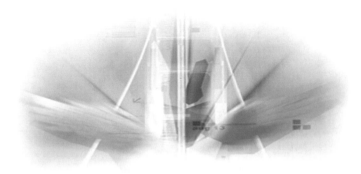

15. Angels and the end

Please read: Matthew 13:36-43, 47-51; 16:27; 25:31-34, 41, 46; Mark 8:38; Luke 9:26; 2 Thessalonians 1:6-8; Revelation 5:11-14

I do not doubt for a moment that the angels of God are involved when a believer dies. The Lord Jesus indicated as much when he spoke these words regarding the beggar Lazarus: 'So it was that the beggar died, and was carried by the angels to Abraham's bosom' (Luke 16:22).

But the end with which we are dealing is not the death of the individual believer. It rather consists of various 'end-time' events. We might say that these events begin with the second coming of the Lord Jesus Christ and culminate in the eternal destruction of the lost and the eternal glory of the saints.

The verses above deal with these events. As we examine them, we find that the same angels who play such a prominent part throughout human history will be prominent again in the 'end-time' events.

What do these verses enable us to say about the role of the angels in these events?

Accompanying the Lord Jesus

First, they tell us that angels will accompany the Lord Jesus Christ when he comes at the end of the age (Matthew 16:27; 25:31; Mark 8:38; Luke 9:26). This world has not heard or seen the last of the Lord Jesus. When he ascended to the Father in heaven, his angels promised that he would come again (Acts 1:11). That promise will eventually be fulfilled.

So much time has elapsed since that promise, that many regard it as being empty and void. But the passage of time does not negate the promise. The author of Hebrews affirms:

'For yet a little while,
And he who is coming will come and will not tarry'
(Hebrews 10:37).

We should always remember that much more time passed before the promise of his first coming was fulfilled!

It is not ours to pass judgement on when the Lord Jesus should come. It is ours to be patient 'until the coming of the Lord' (James 5:7). His coming at the end will be totally unlike his first coming. His first coming was as a mere babe. His second coming will be as the Lord of glory.

His first coming attracted only the attention of a few. His second coming will be noticed by all. The apostle John says: 'Behold, he is coming with clouds, and every eye will see him, even they who pierced him' (Revelation 1:7). Because of the glory with which the Lord Jesus will come, it is not surprising that the angels will accompany him.

The glory of God is to angels what honey is to flies. Angels are always present when God puts his glory on display. We can say, therefore, that God will use the angels to demonstrate the majesty and dignity of the second coming of Christ.

> His first coming was as a mere babe. His second coming will be as the Lord of glory.

Separating

On the basis of the verses above, we can also say that the angels will engage in a work of separation. This work raises important questions.

Who will be separated from whom?

The answer is that the wicked will be separated from the righteous. The Lord Jesus himself stated it very plainly: 'So it will be at the end of the age. The angels will come forth, separate the wicked from among the just...' (Matthew 13:49).

What will result from this act of separation?

The answer is as clear as the noonday sun. For some there will be a 'furnace of fire' and 'wailing and gnashing of teeth'

(Matthew 13:42). For others there will be a shining forth 'as the sun' (Matthew 13:43).

As a result of this act of separation, some will hear God say: 'Come … inherit the kingdom prepared for you from the foundation of the world…' (Matthew 25:34). But others will hear him say: 'Depart from me, you cursed, into the everlasting fire prepared for the devil and his angels…' (Matthew 25:41).

One of the most pointed and graphic references to the doom of the wicked is found in Revelation 14:19: 'So the angel thrust his sickle into the earth and gathered the vine of the earth, and threw it into the great winepress of the wrath of God.'

All of this tells us that life in this world is not all there is. Many would have us to believe it is the case. They tell us that we are nothing more than animals — yes, very sophisticated animals, but still animals! They tell us that we are products of evolution, that we live and die and that is the end of us.

How very different is the message of the Bible! It tells us that we were made by the eternal God as eternal beings. We do not cease to exist when this life ends but rather move from this temporal realm into the eternal realm.

There is something inside each and every one of us that tells us this is true, and nothing can entirely silence that voice or erase that consciousness. The secularists have been trying for years to hammer home the notion that we are creatures only of this temporal realm. But a voice still whispers within: 'You were made for eternity.'

Now we come to the most important and vital question of all.

Who are the wicked and who are the just?

We must be careful how we answer this question. Some of the verses which we are considering give the impression that a person's eternal destiny is determined by his works. Do more good things than bad, and you're in!

But the Bible is very emphatic that we can never be saved by our works but only by faith in the redeeming work of Christ. The apostle Paul puts it bluntly: 'For by grace you have been saved through faith, and that not of yourselves; it is the gift of God, not of works, lest anyone should boast' (Ephesians 2:8-9).

Paul makes the same point by referring to Abraham: 'For if Abraham was justified by works, he has something to boast about ... For what does the Scripture say? "Abraham believed God, and it was accounted to him for righteousness." Now to him who works, the wages are not counted as grace but as debt. But to him who does not work but believes on him who justifies the ungodly, his faith is accounted for righteousness...' (Romans 4:2-5).

Salvation resides, then, not in our works but in the Lord Jesus. He is ever the dividing line for the human race! The apostle John declares: '...God has given us eternal life, and this life is in his Son. He who has the Son has life; he who does not have the Son of God does not have life' (1 John 5:11-12).

The Bible is equally emphatic that while works cannot save us, they can and do indicate whether we are saved. They cannot give us a relationship to Christ, but they indicate whether we have that relationship (Ephesians 2:10).

The wicked are those who show by their lives that they do *not* know the Lord Jesus Christ as their Saviour. And the righteous are those who show by their lives that they *do* know the Lord Jesus Christ.

Worshipping

We can go yet further on this matter of the angels' role at the end, namely, they will join the saints in worship of the Lord Jesus Christ. This truth was revealed to the apostle John. After relating the worship of the saints of God (Revelation 5:8-10), John writes: 'Then I looked, and I heard the voice of many angels around the throne, the living creatures, and the elders; and the number of them was ten thousand times ten thousand, and thousands of thousands, saying with a loud voice:

"Worthy is the Lamb who was slain
To receive power and riches and wisdom,
And strength and honour and glory and blessing!"'
(Revelation 5:11-12).

We have already established that the angels desire to look into salvation (1 Peter 1:12). We should not be surprised, therefore, to find them offering praise and worship to God when salvation's work is finally complete.

When the end begins to unfold, we will at long last see the angels with whom so many have been so intrigued and infatuated. But they will not be the primary object of our attention. It will rather be the Lord Jesus Christ. Those who have believed in him will with bursting hearts pour forth praise to him for saving them. And those who have rejected him will deeply regret their decision.

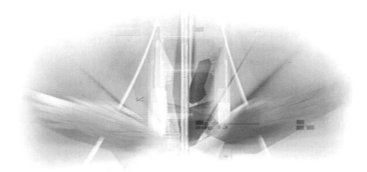

16. The last appearance of an angel in the Bible

Please read: Revelation 22:6-11

We are not looking at the last appearance of an angel in the Bible because it is last. There is no particular significance to that. We are rather examining it because of the significance of what the angel said. It is a message that has not faded with the passing of time. It is one that is as fresh and meaningful as it was when the angel first declared it.

This message consists of four parts: an assurance (v. 6), a quotation (v. 7), a rebuke (vv. 8-9) and an instruction (vv. 10-11).

An assurance (v. 6)

The book of Revelation may very well be the most remarkable book in the Bible. Through a series of astonishing visions, it

> The Lord Jesus Christ and all those who belong to him will finally prove to be victorious.

drives home one unrelenting message: the Lord Jesus Christ and all those who belong to him will finally prove to be victorious.

It was a message that the early Christians sorely needed, and it is one that we need as well. It so often seems that the devil is winning. But that is in appearance only. Our Christ will finally prove to be the conquering Christ, and every knee will eventually bow before him and every tongue will confess that he is Lord.

The visions given to John were of such an astounding nature that he might very well have found them difficult to believe. Could such things really be true? The angel assured him that they were. Richard Brooks writes:

We have read many strange things, many amazing things, many delightful things and many terrible things in this book. But one thing is sure: everything we have read is true — all the messages of salvation, all the warnings of judgement, all the statements about history! 'Trustworthy and true' are two great words that characterize everything about God's Word.[1]

The fact that John took the angel's message to his heart is proven by his own warning that no one should add to or take from what he had written.

In confirming the truth of the book of Revelation, the angel also virtually affirmed the truth of all Scripture. The same God who gave John this revelation was the God of 'the holy prophets' (v. 6), and Scripture is 'the prophetic word' (2 Peter 1:19). The apostle's warning about adding to or taking from the book of Revelation can be extended, therefore, to all Scripture.

Have we, like John, taken the truth about Scripture to our hearts? Or do we add to it our own traditions and new revelations? Or, on the other hand, do we try to tone down what it says about sin, judgement and the redeeming work of Christ as the only possible way of salvation?

This much is clear — if we want to honour the angels with whom we are so enamoured, we will honour the Word of God!

A quotation (v. 7)

Having assured John of the truthfulness of what he had written, the angel shares with him some words from the Lord Jesus himself. These words consist of two parts: the promise that the Lord Jesus will come quickly, and the pronouncement of blessing upon the one who orders his life in accordance with the teaching of Revelation.

The word 'quickly' means, first, that the Lord will come soon; and, secondly, that his coming will be sudden, that is, 'in a moment, in the twinkling of an eye' (1 Corinthians 15:52). We have no difficulty with the latter, but we wonder how the former can be true. Almost two thousand years have come and gone since the angel quoted these words! How can this be a quick coming?

The answer lies in God's different perspective on time. What seems very long to us is only a brief moment to him. If a thousand years is to the Lord as a single day (2 Peter 3:8), less than two days have passed since this promise was given to John! Verses such as this one are not given to us to encourage speculation about when the Lord will come but rather to spur us to live obediently so that we will be ready when he does come.

This, of course, is the truth driven home by the second part of the angel's quotation: 'Blessed is he who keeps the words of the prophecy of this book' (Revelation 22:7). The devil has so blinded the minds of people that very few these days attach blessedness or happiness to obedience to God. The words of Jesus set the record straight! And our own experience confirms them! Wrecked bodies, ruined relationships and various addictions are proof enough of the heavy price of sin.

A rebuke (vv. 8-9)

The apostle John was so overwhelmed with the 'heavy-duty' nature of what he had seen and heard that he 'fell down to worship before the feet of the angel' (v. 8). That was not the right thing to do, and the angel wasted no time in letting John know it: 'See that you do not do that' (v. 9). The angel knew what so many these days do not know, namely, worship belongs to God and God alone (v. 9). When we give to angels what belongs to God, we insult both the angels and God!

The angel was not to receive worship because he was not God. He was rather John's fellow servant and the fellow servant of all the prophets.

While the good angels, then, are higher beings than ourselves, they have the same function. They serve God. The great difference is that they do so perfectly and we imperfectly. We honour the angels, therefore, not by worshipping them, but rather by faithfully serving the God whom they love and adore.

An instruction (vv. 10-11)

After rebuking John, the angel instructed him to leave the book of Revelation unsealed. This stands in contrast with the instruction Daniel received centuries before. He was told to 'seal up the vision' he had received. The reason was that 'it refers to many days in the future' (Daniel 8:26).

The fact that John was given the opposite instruction shows us that the things he had written were urgently needed at that time. The prophecy was not to be sealed and kept for later. It was to be shared. Urgent need was to be met with diligent proclamation!

The words of verse 11 are variously interpreted. The words 'let him be'

> We honour the angels ... not by worshipping them but rather by faithfully serving the God whom they love and adore.

113

must certainly not be taken to mean that the angel was giving permission for people to be 'unjust' or 'filthy'.

Some understand the angel to be referring to those who are so hardened and entrenched in their sins that God, as an act of judgement, was saying: 'Let them be.' William Hendricksen paraphrases the verse in this way: 'Do not hinder the man who, in spite of all pleadings, admonitions, exhortations, etc., has completely hardened himself in his wickedness.'[2]

But the preceding phrase 'the time is at hand' (v. 10) emphasizes the urgency of the truth which God had revealed to John. In light of that urgency, we can paraphrase the angel's message in this way: 'Eternity is so rapidly approaching that the unjust and filthy have only a brief moment to break with their sins. If they do not seize that moment, they must remain for ever in their sins, even as the righteous and holy will remain for ever in their righteousness.'

Life seems to be long to us, but this life is short and eternity is long! At its very longest, this life gives us a very brief time to prepare for eternity.

How can we prepare for eternity? How do we make the transition from being 'unjust' and 'filthy' to being 'righteous' and 'holy'? We need not be in suspense about this matter. The Bible makes it abundantly plain that Christ is the way into heaven. He alone has the righteousness that God demands before we can enter into heaven. And his righteousness counts for us when we repent of our sins and put our trust in what the Lord Jesus has done for sinners.

The last appearance of an angel in the Bible is, then, brimming with significance. Through that appearance, the angel made these truths very plain:

The last appearance of an angel in the Bible

- the Word of God is true
- the Lord Jesus is coming
- God alone is to be worshipped
- our spiritual condition is a matter of extreme urgency.

This passage enables us to say that the angels passed off the stage of the Bible by pointing us, not to themselves, but rather to the things that matter most. Let us heed their message.

Notes

Chapter 1 — The God of the angels
1. Cited by David Jeremiah, *Angels: The Host of Heaven*, Walk Thru the Bible Ministries, p.14.
2. As above, p.12.
3. As above, pp.12-3.

Chapter 2 — The résumé of Lucifer
1. Jonathan Edwards, *The Works of Jonathan Edwards*, The Banner of Truth Trust, vol. ii, p.609.
2. As above.
3. As above, p.610.

Chapter 3 — At war with Satan
1. Cited by Geoffrey B. Wilson, *Ephesians*, The Banner of Truth Trust, p.130.

Chapter 4 — What the cherubim have to say
1. Derek Thomas, *God Strengthens*, Evangelical Press, p.27.

Chapter 6 — In the school of the seraphim

1. Jeremiah, *Angels*, p.36.
2. R. C. Sproul, *The Holiness of God*, Tyndale House Publishers, Inc., p.46.
3. As above.

Chapter 7 — Gabriel, God's preaching angel

1. A similar chapter appears in my book *The 31 Days of Christmas*, Evangelical Press, pp.19-24.
2. Herschel H. Hobbs, *Fundamentals of Our Faith*, Broadman Press, p.45.

Chapter 8 — Michael, the archangel

1. Stuart Olyott, *Dare to Stand Alone*, Evangelical Press, p.132.
2. Stephen R. Miller, *The New American Commentary: Daniel*, Broadman & Holman Publishers, p.285.
3. Cited by Miller, *Daniel*, p.290.

Chapter 9 — The Angel of the Lord

1. Cited by Ron Rhodes, *Angels Among Us*, Harvest House Publishers, p.112.

Chapter 10 — Jesus, lower than the angels

1. John Owen, *An Exposition of the Epistle to the Hebrews*, Baker Book House, vol. iii, p.359.

Chapter 11 — Jesus, higher than the angels

1. Philip Edgcumbe Hughes, *A Commentary on the Epistle to the Hebrews*, William B. Eerdmans Publishing Company, p.55.

2. Geoffrey B. Wilson, *Hebrews*, The Banner of Truth Trust, p.23.

Chapter 12 — Angels as ministering spirits

1. Wilson, *Hebrews*, p.28.
2. John Calvin, *Institutes of the Christian Religion*, The Westminster Press, vol. i, p.167.
3. William Hendriksen, *New Testament Commentary: Matthew*, Baker Book House, p.693.
4. John MacArthur Jr, *The MacArthur New Testament Commentary: Matthew 16-23*, Moody Press, p.119.

Chapter 13 — Entertaining angels

1. R. Kent Hughes, *Preaching the Word: Hebrews*, Crossway Books, vol. ii, p.210.
2. John MacArthur, *The MacArthur New Testament Commentary: Hebrews*, Moody Press, p.426.

Chapter 14 — Angels desiring to look into salvation

1. A similar chapter appears in my book *The 31 Days of Christmas*, Evangelical Press, pp.13-18.

Chapter 16 — The last appearance of an angel in the Bible

1. Richard Brooks, *The Lamb is all the Glory*, Evangelical Press, pp.196-7.
2. William Hendriksen, *More than Conquerors*, Baker Book House, p.252.

Other titles from the author...

Hold your course

22 daily readings from the book of Colossians

Paul's letter to the Colossians is extremely relevant for today. The church is still assaulted with heresies of all kinds: heresies that call into question the authority of Jesus Christ, the sufficiency of the once-for-all sacrifice of Christ, and the ever-present desire to 'improve' the gospel to make it attractive to the unbelieving world. Roger Ellsworth will guide you through Paul's letter and show you how to apply its truths in your life. You will be challenged, instructed and encouraged to 'hold your course' through the storms of modern life — all the while remaining faithful to the Christ of the Scriptures.

Evangelical Press, ISBN 0-85234-592-5, 208 pages.

Moses

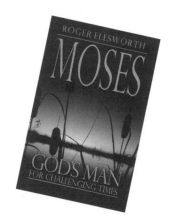

God's man for
challenging times

Moses was God's man for challenging times. In spite of fierce persecution and immense frustration, Moses was able, by the grace of God, to lead the people of Israel from utter despondency to the borders of the promised land. Though thousands of years later, our day is ripe with challenges to the gospel. We can therefore learn from Moses' life. We can learn what it means to walk closely with God day by day; we can learn what it means to find our all-sufficiency in the God of the Bible as we live through sometimes dreary and troublesome times. Further, it is the Christian's great comfort that the Redeemer of Israel is the same today as he was in the days and life of Moses.

Evangelical Press, ISBN 0-85234-586-0, 256 pages.

Be patient, God hasn't finished with me yet!

Learning from the life of Jacob

Jacob lived a very long time ago. There were no computers. Jacob did not send or receive e-mail. There were no television sets, no VCRs, and no cars. What possible value is there, then, in studying the life of a man so far removed from our own sophisticated times?

Simply because Jacob is a picture of us all. It is apparent that he was a deeply flawed man, completely wrapped up in himself and willing to trample on anyone to achieve his own ends. Yet here we see that despite Jacob's failings, God's grace was even greater, and the same grace that worked in the life of Jacob is at work today.

Evangelical Press, ISBN 0-85234-524-0, 128 pages.

A wide range of excellent books on spiritual subjects is available from Evangelical Press. Please write to us for your free catalogue or contact us by e-mail.

Evangelical Press
Faverdale North, Darlington, Co. Durham, DL3 0PH, England

e-mail: sales@evangelicalpress.org

Evangelical Press USA
P. O. Box 825, Webster, New York 14580, USA

e-mail: usa.sales@evangelicalpress.org

web: http://www.evangelicalpress.org